Praise from Parents and

"A revolution is underway in the diagnosis and treatment of autistic spectrum disorders. The leaders of the revolutionary movement have come from unexpected places. They have no advanced medical degrees, no careers in the field, no government funding or institutional standing. But they have power sources of their own. They love their children. They are fiercely determined to find the causes underlying their children's illness and to help them get well. They also have full access to each other and the medical libraries of the world through the Internet. With those formidable powers, they are taking the initiative away from the bureaucracies that have failed their children and are now developing the treatment strategies of the future.

Victoria Beck and her husband Gary have been at the vanguard of the movement. They are inspirations for all parents who struggle with this disorder. Victoria has written an extraordinary book about her life at the front lines of the revolution. If you have an autistic child, you have no choice but to read it. If you are interested in the management of complex disorders like autism, you simply must read it. If you want to know more about the forces affecting the future of medical research in the information age, there is no better case study. The old boundaries are being blown to bits. Nothing will ever be the same."

~ Mark F. Blaxill,
Father of a three-year-old daughter who is on the road to recovery.

"Autism is a kaleidoscopically complex physiological malady. With candor, courage and exquisite intellect, Ms. Beck is victorious once again. Speaking from the trenches, Victoria empowers parents and *health providers to constantly question observations, embrace and organize the medical chaos and realize the reversibility of what once was previously thought to be an irreversible mental illness! Genius is reading and seeing what everyone else does, and thinking about it differently. Victoria is a rare jewel in medicine – a genius and a spiritual person. Parents will cry as they read and realize their pain is heard. Parents will feel empowered to realize they too have contributions to make because they are the experts on their child."*

~ Roberta Olivia Morgan, M.D.

"Confronting Autism: The Aurora on the Dark Side of Venus" is the book I wish someone could have handed to me when my son was diagnosed with autism. It is a remarkable and inspiring book that speaks volumes to the incredible importance and wisdom of a mother's intuition with regard to her sick child. This is the first book that I have read which combines the courageous story of a mother's fight to rescue her child from autism, and the tools that she has developed and implemented to not only help her son, but keep her life balanced and her entire family intact. In her book, Victoria Beck provides us with an invitation to defy probability and statistics and to collectively change the history of autism. It is an invitation too tangible to resist. Victoria Beck's Plan for Empowerment is a strategy that we can all use, no matter when our children were labeled autistic. In fact, the tools she provides in her book transcend autism, and would no doubt be useful to any parent with a special needs child."

~ Ricci Carole Hedequist,
Mother of four, one with autism.

"Mother saves child. Figuratively, Victoria Beck could have been running through the flames of a burning house, but in fact she was reading, talking with other parents and finding doctors to try some rational new interventions for her autistic son. She departed from the old ideas and started thinking about the role of nutrition and intestinal function in behavior, and thousands of other parents have seen success by taking the same path. I am one such parent.

This is a call to action for the parents of autistic children and children with other behavioral disorders to save their kids by visiting the progressive frontiers of medicine. Nutrition and intestinal function matter greatly in these disorders. Hooray! for Victoria Beck in pointing us the way."

~ Woody McGinnis, M.D.

"I am almost at a loss for words. You have taken the journey that we all must face, and put it so eloquently and understandably on paper. I can only state now what I have stated before – you, like many other wonderful parents of children like ours, were put here for a reason. You have begun the map of the road that will be traveled in future years. For that, all of the current, past, and unfortunately future parent advocates for their autistic children will be eternally grateful. You are amazing."

~ Eric Einbinder
Father of two children, one with autism.

Confronting Autism: The Aurora on the Dark Side of Venus

A Practical Guide to Hope, Knowledge, and Empowerment

Victoria A. Beck

New Destiny Educational Products, Inc.
188 Route 101
The Great American Office
Suite 314
Bedford, NH 03110

Printed in the United States of America

ISBN 0-9674969-0-X

To Jordan Elizabeth and James Parker,
with my love, forever.

Disclaimer

This book describes certain information about autism and the emotions and experiences of some people within the autism community. Although portions of this book discuss current research and therapies (medical and otherwise), all such information is to be used only with the guidance of the reader's physicians, nutritionists or other licensed healthcare providers. Some treatments and therapies are new and may be associated with risks that may not be realized for many years to come. Every reader must exercise their own judgement and act on information contained herein only at their own risk. The ideas, opinions and material discussed in this book is offered in the spirit of helping others and does not constitute medical, psychological or educational advice. The author of this book relates certain personal experiences regarding certain treatment regimens in autism but makes no claim that such treatment is appropriate for any other individual. Children with autism differ considerably, and every parent must determine appropriate treatment for his or her autistic child with licensed healthcare providers.

Acknowledgments

Five years ago, my nightstand was adorned with issues of *Bon Appetit* and *Colonial Homes* Magazines. My personal notebooks were filled with clippings of the latest recipes and decorating ideas. Then came autism. Since then, Gary and the children depend largely on take-out if they want a gourmet meal! Eighteenth-century furniture and drapery designs are the furthest thing from my mind. These things and practically everything else has changed since Parker became ill.

My nightstand now sports stacks of medical abstracts and physiology books. My personal notebooks are overflowing with the names and phone numbers of other parents facing autism, researchers, doctors and therapists. All, in what seemed like the blink of a tear-filled eye.

Obviously, if I could trade in autism for the healthy normal child behind it, I would do it in a heartbeat. The special people that autism has put in my path, however, I hope to keep in my life forever. Thank you,

> ...to Dr. Bernard Rimland, whose dedication to the cause of autistic children around the world is beyond comprehension. For over four decades, you have tirelessly committed yourself and your life to autism and have maintained the highest standards of integrity along the way. Thousands of parents and their autistic children are indebted to you for the trail you have blazed. Your knowledge of autism and experience within the autism community are unparalleled. Dr. Rimland, your advice to me is greatly valued and your trust in me will be forever treasured.

…to Dr. Dennis Remmington, for believing in me and for *truly* caring for Parker and our family. We cannot begin to fully express our appreciation for your guidance and your respect. You humbly embody the essence of wisdom and character, and exemplify how medicine should be practiced.

…to Dr. David Gregg, you are a brilliant and compassionate scientist who, despite the chasm between your wealth of scientific knowledge and my dearth of it, never ever try to make me feel inadequate. I am indebted to you for the hours of time you devote to my hours of "whys." You are a humanitarian and a fine human being.

…to Kathy Voltz, my friend whom I have never yet met. You taught me that autism doesn't have to defeat me, and reached out to me, a total stranger, at the lowest point in my life. You inspired me to never give up. Kathy, your sense of humor and positive attitude have been invaluable gifts on some rocky pathways.

…to Ricci Hedequist, my friend and trusted confidant and fellow home-school mom, on whom I have laid lots of laughter and a few tears as well. You are one of the finest people the Internet has ever introduced to me. You have shared your knowledge and your heart willingly and have never put your ego in front of the goal. I respect your insights on autism, and cherish the corner of my heart with you in it.

…to Dr. Woody McGinnis, who has unselfishly spent dozens of hours on the telephone with me (our long-distance carrier loves you), and who has taught me to think in "broad strokes." Thank you for your faith, encouragement, and kindness.

...to doctors and professionals, dedicated to determining the biological causes of autism: Dr. Sidney Baker, Dr. Roberta Olivia Morgan, Dr. Paul Hart, and many, many others. You are a rare group of professionals and the autism community needs you, (and more just like you). Don't give up.

...to friends and fellow parents too numerous to mention, in particular Eric Einbinder, Lisa Mayberry, Dr. Ken Sokolski, Dr. Nancy LeGendre, Rick Rollens, Laura Bono, Mark Blaxill, and Shelly Reynolds. Bright, honest, forward thinking parents like you will drive the direction of the autism community in the years ahead and will generate positive change.

...to Parker's "Dream Team" at our school district – Ken Williams, Heather White, Sue Jones, Dr. Alan Schnee, Jane Cummings, and his therapists – Karen Hagstrom, Amy Christopher, Maria Calabrese, and Kara Reagon. You have demonstrated the kind of dedication to Parker's education that every single autistic child across this nation so desperately needs. We are deeply appreciative and hope that you are further empowered by Parker's progress to continue to do the right thing in the years ahead for Parker and other children like him. My special thanks goes to Kristine Milner, Parker's ABA therapist and guardian angel for over 3 years. Your dedication and love for Parker are extraordinary. God answered a major prayer when he sent you to our doorstep.

...to Dr. Walter Herlihy, who may be the brightest individual I've ever known, and in whom I have the utmost confidence to unravel the connection between secretin and autism. I know that your dedication to autistic children and to quality biomedical research are passionate. Your wisdom, character, and intelligence will help to lead the autism community to a new and higher standard of scientific investigation.

My deepest gratitude goes to my husband and children, my life partners and teammates, whose unfailing support and love are deeply cherished.

Gary, there are no adequate words to thank you for being there every step of the way. For being strong when I was not, for never yielding once to a moment of doubt or negativity. For your unwavering positive belief that if we continued to ask the right questions and remained focused, we would find new hope for Parker. Thank you for typing these words and all of the words of our educational materials until late into the night. For being the consummate father, husband, soul mate and friend. I am grateful I met you on Earth and even more grateful to have had you by my side, every moment, on Venus. In either scenario, you are out of this world! This book, and everything else we do, wouldn't happen without you.

To Jordan Elizabeth, my daughter, you have been my teacher and my mentor in life. The innocence and wonder with which you approach each day is pure and unspoiled, and in following your lead, I have learned the merits of starting my own thought processes at "the beginning." Every day, you ask the most fundamental of life's questions and have, by your example, taught me to re-examine the fundamental truths about autism. In your eyes, I have seen the love for Parker that is often so difficult for us adults to give. You offer love that has no sense of fear or expectation. I strive to be more like you every day. You are already naturally empowered and will continue to refine my empowerment in this cause.

Finally, to Parker. In you, God has made me realize a strength, a commitment and a love I never knew was inside of me. In your eyes I see the boy beneath the behavior. In your life, I have found the inspiration behind this text. In my empowerment, I have finally found you.

About this Book:
A Message of Introduction

A non-verbal, autistic child suddenly speaks and says "mommy" for the first time after being infused with secretin, an intestinal peptide hormone historically used only to diagnose pancreatic function.

Another autistic child barely escapes a life-threatening medical emergency because the doctors in the local hospital refuse to believe that a 102° temperature is a sign of serious infection in this child, whose basal body temperature is always several degrees sub-normal.

Still another child completely recovers from their diagnosis of autism after his parents implement a special diet which restricts proteins from grains and cows milk and which provides extra nutrients and vitamins to the child. The child had suffered for months on end from extreme gastrointestinal discomfort, but no healthcare provider was willing to accept that the physical symptoms were connected to the child's autistic behavior.

A perfectly normal and beautiful little girl is given a well-baby check at her pediatrician's office, during which a mandatory childhood vaccination is administered. Two months later, her smiles are gone, her normal development is arrested, she throws her head back in high pitched screams, and develops chronic diarrhea. Her parents question the pediatrician about whether the sudden onset of her problems are due to the vaccine she received, but the questions are dismissed. Months later, the little girl is diagnosed with autism.

Unfortunately, these are familiar stories to many parents in the autism community. An increasing number of children are being diagnosed with autism and many of them have physiological problems, the onset of which seemed to coincide with their abnormal behavior and "autistic" manifestations. An increasing number of parents are questioning the medical and psychological professionals about the possible biological causes of autism in their children, and question they should.

Part I of this book is a critical look at the premise of autism itself, and the debilitating cycle of hopelessness it generates. It is also a discussion about the positive transformation that can take place for parents and their ill children when knowledge, wisdom and truth in science are sought by all who comprise the body of the autism community.

Part II presents a philosophical and pragmatic look at the plan that my husband Gary and I have used to break the cycle of hopelessness for our child. It comprises the eight steps we designed that eventually led us to the discovery of secretin treatment in autism, a therapy which has not only helped our son, but hundreds of other children worldwide since our story was aired on national television in October 1998. This book *is not* about any one particular treatment or approach for every autistic child. This book *is* about working through the enormous and overwhelming responsibilities of life with autism. It is about challenging the myths about autism that have limited biomedical research and treatment for decades. It is about changing the entire way we look at autism. It is about hope, empowerment and progress.

Foreword

Victoria Beck's book is a treasure – the work of an inspired, and inspiring, highly articulate and remarkably insightful writer. What she says – and says so well – has needed saying for a long time. I fervently hope, and fully expect, that fellow parents of autistic children will pay close heed to Victoria's heartfelt message.

It has been said that the parents of autistic children are the most severely oppressed minority group in America. As a fellow parent (my son Mark is 37 years older than Victoria's son Parker) I have for nearly four decades been urging parents to reject the conventional views that little can be done to help autistic children, and that parents must passively accept the harmful drugs that are the mainstay of the medical profession's approach to autism. I am truly delighted that Victoria is offering parents similar advice and offering them, far more importantly, a practical, step-by-step, easy-to-implement "battle plan" they can use to cut through the red tape, confusion, and politics that stand between their children and real help. Her detailed advice is invaluable – a "crash course" of practical information that most parents spend years learning. Equally important, however, is her inspiring message: that parents possess wisdom and competence, and that they have the right – in fact the obligation – to challenge the fatalistic view of autism held by so many professionals.

Victoria and her husband Gary rejected that view, and, as a result, their son has made remarkable progress toward a normal life. Victoria's story about how they single-handedly discovered the benefits of secretin, and the challenges they faced from the medical community as a result, may seem more like a TV melodrama than a real-life story, but it is all very real. So is the story of how they persevered and shared their discovery with other parents.

The discovery of the effects of secretin on autism plays a major role in this book. During the past several years I have heard from hundreds of families and physicians, including physicians who are themselves parents of autistic children, about the remarkable effects of secretin upon many autistic children. I have encountered no treatment modality, in my 40 years of experience, which is nearly as promising as secretin. We are just at the beginning of learning what the true potential of this hormone may be, not only in the treatment of autism, but, I am confident, in the treatment of a large number of other neurological and metabolic disorders.

We have come a long way – but not nearly far enough – from the day in 1958 when my wife and I, having ourselves diagnosed our severely affected 2-year-old son Mark as being autistic, learned to our horror and dismay that every textbook on psychiatry proclaimed autism to be a "psychogenic" disorder, a mental illness caused by parents who supposedly harbored feelings of hostility toward their child, who was assumed to be biologically normal. This pernicious idea, which was supported by not one shred of scientific evidence, was not presented as a mere theory, or as a hypothesis, but as an unquestioned fact. My book *Infantile Autism*, published in 1964, is credited with destroying that evil myth and establishing autism as a biological disorder. But that was only part of the problem.

After completing *Infantile Autism*, I began a search for effective treatments. I learned about behavior modification (now called "ABA") from Ivar Lovaas in late 1964. The autism professionals scoffed. Ignoring the fact that it obviously worked, they rejected the idea that a technique that was used to train dogs and seals could help autistic children. They would become mere "robots," it was argued. I responded by founding, in 1965, the Autism Society of America, a parent group strong enough to insist that the children receive structured special education, and not just drugs and "play therapy."

In the mid 1960's I also learned about treatment with high-dose vitamin B6 and magnesium. Between 1966 and 1996, 18 studies were published by researchers in 6 countries, showing the B6/magnesium treatment to be far better and safer than any of the available drugs. Eleven of the studies were double-blind, placebo-controlled experiments. Yet the professionals still scoffed, ignoring the evidence and deceiving the parents by claiming there were no scientific studies, or that there were studies that showed the treatment to be useless or harmful. To this day they continue to tell parents the same nonsense.

All the while some of these autism professionals were administering drugs that *were* harmful, conducting research aimed at enhancing their professional status rather than helping the children, and ignoring the emerging research on unpopular or politically incorrect topics, such as vaccine damage and the effects of dietary gluten and casein on autism.

But there were – and are – some excellent, open-minded physicians and researchers really interested in helping autistic children. In January, 1995 I convened our first Defeat Autism Now! (DAN!) Conference in Dallas. The attendees were 30 hand-picked physicians and researchers from the US and Europe. Things have moved quickly since then.

Victoria Beck was a featured speaker at The Autism Research Institute's 4th Annual Defeat Autism Now! Conference held in Cherry Hill, New Jersey in early October, 1998. Her talk was the first public presentation on the autism/secretin connection. As reported in our newsletter, *The Autism Research Review International:*

> *The highlight of the conference was the impassioned address by parent Victoria Beck, whose account of her uphill struggle to establish the autism-secretin*

connection brought a standing ovation from the crowd of 1,200.

The best, most overwhelming, most articulate talk I've ever heard," said Maureen McDonnell, R.N., coordinator of the conference. Noting that there was hardly a dry eye in the house, McDonnell added, "the next time she speaks, I'll bring boxes of tissues to hand out to the audience.

Victoria's book, however, is not just about secretin – which, as she explains, is just one key to the puzzle of autism, and will not be part of the answer for every autistic child. Instead, she charts a path to help parents of autistic children evaluate the various medical and educational options available. If you are the parent of an autistic child, and the deluge of conflicting treatment information has you feeling overwhelmed and confused, Victoria's book will help you to efficiently and assertively plan the best course of action to maximize your child's potential.

In addition, you will find strength and courage in the story of the Beck's successful battle against seemingly overwhelming odds. And successful it has been.

Parker Beck, the first child to respond to secretin, is doing very well. Several months ago, while the Becks were vacationing in San Diego, we invited them to attend a dinner meeting of the Board of Directors of the Autism Research Institute. The restaurant was able to find us a small private dining room, with a separate table where charming 6-year-old Parker and his delightful 8-year-old sister Jordan could be served their dinner while they worked on their coloring books. A few feet away, we adults dined and conducted our Board meeting. After about 20 minutes, little Parker got up from his chair and came over to the adult's table, where he handed one note to his mother Victoria and another to his father Gary. Victoria and Gary each unfolded their notes and broke into pleased smiles. Parker had handed each of them a carefully folded drawing on which was printed very carefully and neatly the words "I love you mommy" and "I love you daddy."

I will never forget that incident. It made worthwhile all the years of hard work and all the sacrifice endured by Gary and Victoria, and the others of us at the table. Victoria's brilliant and dedicated efforts to help other parents will, I'm sure, result in equally heartening scenes being enacted in future years, in many thousand of homes worldwide.

Bernard Rimland, Ph.D.
The Autism Research Institute
San Diego, CA

September, 1999

Prologue

The exact date escapes me, but I remember that first day my sister got on the phone with me and said, "Brian, there's something *wrong* with Parker."

Victoria and I had always been very close. Through the years, in our darkest moments, we had consoled each other and guided one another through those various life crises in which people invariably find themselves. It is not currently politically correct, but I have generally found the female of the species to be at least outwardly more emotional than the male. Having said that, when seeking advice from Victoria, I always found her level-headed and emotionally restrained. I had seen her weather a number of difficult challenges with grace, bury both parents at too young an age, and suffer the throes of a colicky first child with patience and understanding.

But I had never heard her voice sound quite like it did that day. I tried to console her, yet I knew that she would not have called me and made that statement unless weeks or months of experience with Parker had progressively convinced her that indeed something was wrong. In this book, Victoria describes autism as being something of a contagion – a contagion of the soul and spirit. I felt the impact of that contagion right there on the phone, in her voice…a cold omen of the future.

An unattached bachelor for a quarter of a century, I thought I had come to know the meaning of the word "alone." Holidays can be tough, as can extended family picnics when you have no family or children of your own. When problems at work arise, there is no one at home to faithfully support you.

Yet, autism has taught me that I didn't really know "alone" after all.

The disappointment, the shock, the denial, the pain, the frustration, the confusion, the misinformation, the omnipresence of this disease have left whole generations of parents truly alone. Victoria and Gary were two of the strongest and most organized individuals I knew. Their marriage was, by today's standards, extraordinarily happy and secure, and they were going places. Gary was a hard-driving up-and-comer in the banking industry and Victoria was a devoted full-time mom. She home schooled her first born and was totally dedicated to her children and husband. Within a year of Parker's disease, their lives were turned upside down. No more normal socializing with friends and family. No more breakable knick-knacks on display in the house. Extra locks on the doors from the inside out. No more restaurants on a hot summer day. No more normal meal times. Being ignored by people who were unwilling to look at autism in the eye. Lack of time. Lack of sleep. Lack of answers. No answers. No help.

They were starkly alone.

Making this situation even worse was the fact that Victoria wasn't really *ever* alone, at least not in the physical sense. She could never leave Parker out of her sight. He never seemed to lose energy, he never seemed to sleep or slow down. He had no sense of danger. And you could communicate precious little to establish any sort of control. Oh, and, of course, no convenient babysitters; not for a child with autism.

Alone, yet horribly not alone.

My sister was (and is!) a levelheaded, intelligent, strong woman with a great life partner and yet she was reduced to a crying wreck on some nights by the contagion of autism. Day upon week upon month of this unrelenting and seemingly unforgiving condition took one of the strongest people I have known and reduced her almost to a mere shell. The description, however, does read *almost*.

Enough of Victoria's inner strength hung on to drive the pendulum back the other way.

This book is, in part, her story. And though it is, of course, Parker's story as well, the book truly belongs to the autistic community.

It is a book that tells them: you are not alone, or without hope, after all.

Brian James Land
September, 1999

Table of Contents

Part I

Part II

Part I

Chapter One

The Current State of Autism: Astrology for the Modern Culture

*"Life can only be understood backwards;
but it must be lived forwards."*

~ Søren Kierkegaard

Gary and I met in an astronomy class. We were both finishing our last science elective in college. Neither of us had much interest in the class. As the year and our friendship with each other progressed, both of us realized we were not quite as focused on the subject matter being taught as our fellow stargazers were. Looking back, there is no doubt in my mind that during this study of the heavens, the work of angels was subtly taking place. It had been an over-booked course. The professor had made an exception to the rule by allowing Gary to sign up for the late-night class, and in a jam-packed room, the only available seat was next to me. Fate was a friend that day.

I'd like to think that, at the very least, my astronomy class broadened my understanding of the universe and all its properties. Fact is, most of the course material remains a blur. In retrospect, maybe my attention was ever so slightly distracted by Gary's dazzling smile or the smell of his cologne (it still is). For sure, now 13 years later, almost all of the technical information about the wonders in space has left my brain. Whenever I look up in the night sky, I don't think about cosmic rays, supernovae, magnetic fields or quasars. I think about what is clearly in front of my eyes. I think about the stars, plain and simple.

The glorious luster of the stars on a clear night are, at the same time, magnificent and humbling. Magnificent in their brilliance; humbling because they remind us all how much there is waiting to be revealed to us about our universe and how great and elusive the heavens are – even to the finest astronomers and scientists in our world. Indeed, whether one is technically oriented or not, the stars are an important connection to the relatively unexplored existence beyond our planet. For the scientists, the stars hold important clues to the properties of the universe. For more ordinary gazers like me, those stars provide perspective on the world and help to validate the presence of phenomena that is beyond our human understanding.

Years after the two-semester astronomical experience, only one topic remains etched in my brain today. The chapter discussing the planet Venus must have permanently stayed in the recesses of my mind because it was named for the Roman goddess of love, who had paid a personal visit to Gary and me that year. I have since come to realize that, in many ways, those recollections have become a kind of defining point, metaphorically, of our journey into the world of autism with our second child, our son Parker.

Venus (named for the great mother goddess) has been the object of intense interest and scrutiny by astronomers for centuries. Its proximity to our own planet, as well as many of its general characteristics, initially made it seem strikingly similar to Earth. Many of the geological features of Venus are features familiar to Earth. It has mountains, volcanoes, canyons and plains. What *scientists* have come to learn, however, is that at some point in the history of the universe, Earth and Venus took on different forms.[1]

The clouds that completely shroud Venus are, ironically, what make the planet stand out so obviously in the sky. The clouds around Venus reflect the light from the sun. They also hide the planet from the eye of the telescope, and astronomers have had to develop extraordinary methods for penetrating the clouds of Venus in order to learn more about its properties. Special radar techniques have helped scientists to look beyond the exterior cloud cover and unlock the secrets not previously known. In fact, it wasn't until 1961, hundreds of years after Galileo's time, that it was discovered that Venus actually slowly rotates in a direction opposite to that of the other orbital and rotational motions in our solar system. The *retrograde* rotation of Venus is still not understood. However, in the midst of its mysterious and slow retrograde motion, an interesting phenomenon takes place. As the molecules around the planet move to its dark side, they cool down, combine into new molecules with more energy, and begin to emit light. This creates a spectacular sight around the cloud cover. The phenomenon is known in astronomy as the *Aurora on the Dark Side of Venus*.[2]

Children suffering from autism parallel typical children, as Venus parallels Earth. Theirs is a world which, at first glance, seems so close to our own. So near, so similar at first glance, yet so different. Their souls reflect the same light as other children, yet their lives are shrouded in a cloud cover we often cannot penetrate without special techniques. Under the cloud cover, despite their sometimes seemingly mysterious and curious actions, are their magical moments of luminescence, when a word or a connection appears to arise from the darkness. These are the signals which, although sometimes irregular, are undeniable and unmistakable to those of us who love and care about these children. They are the outward signs that let us know that typical children are really there, underneath the cloud cover and within our reach.

There are other parallels between astronomy and autism. Historically, astronomy was largely that which we know today as *astrology*. Even though it was widely popular in its day, astrology was based on myth and irrational preconceived notions; notions that we readily dismiss now, but that in their day were virtually gospel. Astronomy changed dramatically following medieval times. Its entire premise changed, from being a phenomenon worthy of study solely in sociological and psychological circles, into a subject worthy of rational and methodical science. Had the Renaissance not brought with it pioneers such as Copernicus, Galileo and Newton, we might all believe that the laws and physical properties of the world are determined by Zeus himself. These pioneers changed the way that modern scientists look at the universe. They introduced a new valid truth to us all.[3]

For many years, autism had suffered from the myth (promulgated by professionals with impressive credentials) that the condition was caused, among other similar and ridiculous things, by heartless and cold "refrigerator" mothers. It took years before parents (and especially mothers) were able to get beyond the guilt heaped upon them by psychoanalysts like Bruno Bettelheim who promoted these preposterous ideas. We may think we have come far since the days of Bettelheim. Relatively speaking, our modern culture hasn't yet really emerged from the Dark Ages in our view of autism or our approach to exploring it. Much of what is still accepted today, despite evidence to the contrary, is based on the belief that autism is exclusively an incurable psychological disorder, which automatically and forever destines the child affected by it to a second-class life. This cruel myth, creating de-facto second-class juvenile citizens is only exceeded by the third-rate treatment of these same children by many in the educational, psychological, medical and insurance communities.

The rate of autism is increasing dramatically,[4] and a large group of the children with autism today (arguably, the vast majority of newly diagnosed cases) involve *physiological* abnormalities. The physiological nature of our children's challenges is profoundly obvious to those of us who live with our children on a daily basis. Many of our children have severe gastrointestinal problems. Many are grossly deficient in nutritional elements of one kind or another. They often have symptoms of thyroid disorders, poor muscle tone, abnormal neurological and immunological profiles, and problems with visual perception.

Despite these physiological realities, autism continues to be defined and taught in medical school as a behavioral and mental disorder (according to what I have been told by recent medical school graduates). It is usually attached to the word "lifelong," and the responsibility to find biomedical treatment options is largely left to the child's parents. Such physiological problems in our children are either assumed by much of traditional medicine to be of no significance (and therefore unworthy of exploration) or determined to be independent of the developmental and behavioral issues at hand.

This view has preserved a premise about autism that is as archaic as medieval astrology. The "experts" have apparently reasoned that the lack of grounded, scientific, peer-reviewed, conclusive evidence pointing to one specific biomedical cause for our children's illness, by default preserves the traditional definitions of autism despite the fact that no one has ever proven the traditional views, either. There is one huge fatal flaw in their premise. The lack of evidence proving the underlying biomedical cause or causes of autism does not, by its absence, *prove* that autism is therefore merely behavior or development gone awry. Nor does it prove a purely genetic cause. It is, simply stated, a lack of evidence, or more correctly, *evidence ignored and therefore not yet proved.*

On the surface, this may seem like a minor issue. Nothing could be further from the truth. *Our children will never permanently emerge from the dark ages of autism if we do not do everything within our abilities to change the premise currently accepted by the majority of professionals in the medical and psychological communities.* Calling them worthless and pointless, many of these same professionals have ranted vociferously and railed adamantly about the supposedly unproven medical treatments and procedures we as parents have sought and even demanded. Steadfastly they cleave, all the while, to a definition and a premise about autism which has so many holes in its logic it could not stand the test of even the most primitive scientific rigor. Where are the clinical trials, which would be able to factor *out* biochemical involvement in our children, to isolate it as *solely* a behavioral or developmental disorder? Where are the control groups to prove, beyond a shred of scientific doubt, that the biochemistry of children with autism is identical to that of the norms? Of course, there are no such studies. Nor are there adequate studies to justify the use of psychoactive drugs or high-dose corticosteroids, which carry a fair share of potential and serious adverse side effects. Yet, these kinds of drugs are prescribed daily to our children without hesitation or reservation. Quite a double standard. So why have we, as a parent community, allowed our children to be defined and pigeonholed in such a hopeless, incomplete way? Why have we, as our children's most ardent advocates, endured with more than a fair degree of complacency, the attempts to thwart biomedical research and interventions for our autistic children? Why have we as parents not stood up more confidently and not spoken out more assuredly about the "other" side of autism – the physiological side – the reality of which is overwhelming?

Many children have dramatically improved, or recovered completely, after dietary or medical interventions of one kind or another. These children refute the old myths, and provide the basis for intense scientific and medical scrutiny, toward the goal of a cure. But efforts and support to explore even the most obvious territory fall victim to the comfort zones of bygone eras in autism history and to close-minded attitudes within the medical, psychological and educational professions. In addition, often the most sincere and interested professionals and doctors become trapped in a medical/political system which hails prestigious research institutions as the only entities capable of charting medical progress. The observations and input of parents and fine practitioners are discounted as being meaningless and anecdotal at best. Consequently, our children become trapped in retrograde motion, like Venus.

Instead of trying to delve into the biological causes of autism, we have allowed the mainstream educational, medical and psychological communities to convince us to be complacent. We have, in our complacency, accepted the notion that these beautiful creations somehow either have abnormal brain function, the sudden etiology of which is not proven, have consciously chosen this mysterious, cloud-covered existence of their own volition, or worse, have been put there through the fault of irresponsible parents.

We, as parents, have held these children, have loved them, and have watched them fall asleep in our arms. We know their touch, the sound of their laugh, the smell of their skin. We know so much more about their everyday behaviors, symptoms and changes than that which can be examined in a physician's office or a psychologist's clinic in an hour or a day. We also know that a bright, functioning, loving, beautiful child is underneath all of the untypical behavior. We recognize the little (but very real) breakthroughs that appear spontaneously or after interventions of one kind or another. We know that our children are not hopelessly pre-destined to fail.

Five hundred years ago, forward-looking and open-minded people shed the specter of the kind of pre-destination that astrology proffered its sect of believers. Likewise, for the autistic community today, the time is ripe for the transformation of our thinking, of our acting, and of autism itself. We need a new premise. Our gaze needs to be cast upward and our confidence needs to be magnified in great measure if change, and a chance for our children, is to take place.

Chapter Two

The Challenge:
Getting Beyond the Clouds

*"It's not the situation…
it's your reaction to the situation."*

~ Bob Conklin

Picture this. You go to bed one evening in the way you have always gone to bed. The doors are locked. The house is safe. You have checked on all of the children, and they are peacefully tucked under the covers, sleeping without a stir. You brush your teeth and retire to your bed. As you nod into dreamland, your mind is filled with thoughts of the things tomorrow will bring. Upon awakening, you find, much to your shock and surprise, that you and your family have been transported to an unfamiliar place, quite different and more foreboding than where you went to sleep the night before. You look around, and you are scared. Where are you? You try to figure out where you are and how you got there.

You and your family spend hours looking all around for some clue that will help determine your whereabouts. Perhaps this is just a bad dream, you think to yourself. As you pinch your leg, you rule out that possibility.

In a deep and reflective state of mind, you try to recall whether anyone has ever described a place like this to you before. Your memory does not provide any information that can help you. You summon God for help and guidance. As you feel your heart begin to pound faster and faster within your body, you even begin to bargain with God to show you His presence. If He will only help you now, you will never ask Him for another thing your entire life.

More time passes. You try and reassure yourself and your family that everything will be okay, and that whatever has brought you to this strange place must surely be a passing phenomenon. Tensions among all of you are beginning to escalate, which is not helping to ease the fear of this unknown environment. To make matters worse, one of your children, is acting in a bizarre manner, and your attempts to get him to cooperate with the rest of the family fail miserably. Your daughter is scared, and she begins to cry. You hold her close to comfort her. You are scared. So is your husband.

This foreign place is dark, and thick with an ominous low-lying fog that makes it difficult to see beyond a few feet in any one direction. Still, you believe you catch a glimpse of something just beyond your grasp. You slowly edge your way over to it. Sure enough, it is a rusty old road sign. A road sign must mean that someone has been here before! As you pick up the sign, you think you are a step closer to solving this mystery. The sign reads "VENUS." Whew! Now you know the name for where you are, and you can tell from the age of the sign and the footsteps in the soil all around it, that many other people have been here before as well. You think you are making progress. Your husband shouts out to you. Good news! He has found something else! It's a roadmap and a navigation guide – hooray! It appears, initially, that all may not be lost.

As you crawl back to your husband and children, you sense a glimpse of renewed spirit conquering some of the fear. You have a name for this foreign environment, a roadmap and a navigation guide. Your husband and you are bright, strong people, and you are not easily thwarted in the face of challenge or adversity. Together, you will find your way home.

The map is tattered and faded. Slowly, you unravel it. Sure enough, this map says "VENUS" at the top, but it depicts a series of circles leading nowhere. No wonder someone has tossed it on the ground. In addition, the clouds around you are so thick that you cannot determine what anything is, beyond five feet away. The winds are so strong, they are pulling you in one direction, even though your intuition tells you that you should be headed in a different direction.

The map does not provide you with the guidance you need in this strange place called "Venus." You still have the navigation guide, and perhaps it will be of some help. Your hopes are dashed upon realizing that the navigation guide presumes you have come to Venus to stay permanently, and provides no indication of how to get back home to Earth.

Once again you are scared, you are bewildered, and it appears that you and your family are hopelessly lost. You realize you must somehow journey back to EARTH and have no idea how to get there.

So far, you have three tools at your disposal. A rusty old sign, a useless map, and a navigation guide that doesn't provide the direction you need. You have a family who is unprepared and confused, one child behaving particularly out of control, and no clue as to how this all has happened.

Three main choices await you and your family. You can:

1. Do nothing, and hope that a miracle will return you to the life you once knew.

2. Succumb to resignation, and decide how to best manage and live on this new planet.

3. Get tough, and decide that your will and your fate will not be determined by the few useless tools you have found in this horrible environment, and that you will never abandon your search for a way out.

None of these choices *guarantee* a positive outcome. But, only choice number 3 will provide you with a useful and hopeful strategy.

You cannot be certain of anything except this: you, your husband and children did not choose to be on Venus, and it is an awful and ominous place. You must reach deep within your heart and your mind and gather all of your determination and resourcefulness. You must use all of the knowledge, wisdom, and courage with which you were endowed to find your way home.

Life with autism *is* life on the dark side of Venus. What follows is the story of my family's unexpected journey into the realm of autism, and the plan of empowerment we adopted in response to our situation. Presented with a poor selection of tools to aid us, we developed a plan: ideas, patterns and strategies to transcend the ominous clouds of autism. It resulted in tremendous positive change for our child and us. By sharing our story and our plan, we hope to provide some measure of understanding, comfort, guidance and inspiration to help you and your family move beyond the clouds of autism, too.

Chapter Three

A New Direction:
A Revelation in the Darkness

*"The function of fear is to warn us of danger,
not to make us afraid to face it."*

~ unknown

James "Parker" was born in January 1993 in California, where Gary and I had been living just outside of San Francisco. He was our second child, preceded by the arrival of his sister Jordan, just 22 months earlier.

My pregnancy and delivery with Parker had been flawless, and the early months of Parker's infancy were joyous ones, especially in contrast to the same months of extreme colic we had experienced with his older sister. He was almost always happy and smiling. He slept for long periods at a time. Gary and I used to make jokes about how God must have thought we had paid our "dues" with Jordan's colic, and had blessed us with a contented and easy-spirited son by comparison.

The only thing of concern, upon mental reflection and my review of his baby journal, was a "gurgling" sound, a sort of "rasp" in his breathing which occurred very early on in the first few months, and which lasted for about one year. We had expressed this concern to our California pediatrician, because cystic fibrosis had claimed one of my cousin's children. It seemed that Parker always had an abundance of mucus in his lungs. Our pediatrician assured us that he was not at all worried. All seemed very normal.

Within two months of Parker's birth, we moved to a new home in Seattle. When he was six months of age, I ceased breast-feeding Parker and put him on a milk-based formula. The gurgling problem in his lungs magnified considerably and he began to have bouts of diarrhea. We switched to a soy formula, which seemed to clear his lungs, but left him so terribly constipated, he would cry in pain until we gave him a bottle of milk-based formula which, in turn, always cleared his bowels. Around the same time, Parker received his 4- and 6-month vaccinations, including two rounds of DPT shots (Diphtheria, Pertussis, and Tetanus). Our Seattle pediatrician actually gave both rounds of vaccines only one month apart. He had advised this because Gary's employer would soon transfer us to a new city (Denver), and he thought that by getting Parker's vaccines "out of the way," he would spare us the problem of having to find a new doctor immediately upon our arrival in Colorado.

That was the beginning of a new set of problems. Within days of the vaccines, Parker's cheeks grew red and rashy. He began to have ear infections that persisted, despite endless rounds of antibiotics. He continued to experience episodic diarrhea, which we continued to control by alternating the milk and soy formula. Behaviorally, he continued to be an interactive, happy, alert and "connected" child in every way. He babbled, he cooed, he made every major developmental milestone on time or before schedule. We continued to inquire about the rashy cheeks and the abnormal (and often foul) bowel movements. Everything was dismissed as "typical baby stuff." And, he *was* typical in every way, developmentally, behaviorally, and emotionally.

Life was very busy, but it was very good. Gary and I were immensely grateful to have two beautiful and happy children and to have one another to share the journey with them. Our lives revolved around our family. I loved my role as a stay-at-home-mom, and we both delighted in parenthood.

In May 1994, we learned of yet another job transfer for Gary. This time it would be to Utah. Gary had to leave immediately. He was in Utah for almost four months before we sold our home in Colorado and I was able to move out to be with him. During that four-month period in Utah, Gary traveled home to be with the children and me every weekend. In mid-May, our Colorado pediatrician administered Parker's 15-month MMR (Measles, Mumps, and Rubella) vaccination. Within a week, Parker's diarrhea re-appeared with a vengeance, and we sought a number of treatments for it, all to no avail. Of more importance, was that he seemed a bit out of sorts, more fussy than usual. He didn't sleep as well as he had slept before. He wasn't easily consoled. He began to refuse food, unless we "mesmerized" him in front of a favorite video at mealtime.

We voiced our concerns to our pediatrician and were assured that Parker's problems had absolutely no connection to the vaccine he had been given. We were never told that any kind of form existed to document adverse effects to vaccines. Instead, the pediatrician suggested that perhaps Gary's absence had confused Parker. Perhaps he missed his daddy, and that was the explanation for his curious and rather "aloof" attitude, she suggested. Before long however, our concern became more than casual. His ear infections were in full swing, his diarrhea was chronic, and his interactions with others were almost non-existent. By July 1994, only 2 months post-MMR vaccine, Parker was "zoned out," and not even responding to our calls to him or our presence. All semblance of communication had ceased at his end. He rarely uttered a sound, babbled, or spoke the words he had learned and used so often before his vaccination.

Intermittently, he threw his head back and let out high-pitched screaming sounds.

We arrived on Utah's doorstep, once again seeking a new pediatrician. Parker was due for his 18-month well-baby check, but I was only able to book an appointment 4 weeks in advance. Each passing day fueled our fears about Parker even more. He began to have little "shivering" episodes – usually after eating or naptime (and had no reason to be cold or chilled in July). He began to refuse all of the foods he had happily eaten for months prior to his MMR vaccination, and frequently, instead of eating, would line up his bite-sized pieces of sandwich on his high-chair tray in rows, over and over again.

The toys that had once delighted Parker and entertained his every hour were now of no interest. Instead, he played with a 4-cup electric coffeepot for hours at a time, taking apart the stem, the filter basket, the lid and the cord, and reconnecting them all with great determination. He idled aimlessly around the house, unwilling to be engaged in play, and amused himself by knocking objects off the tables onto the floor, and tipping the kitchen chairs over, again and again and again. Intermittently, he entranced himself by episodes of spinning. It was painfully obvious that something was dreadfully wrong with our little boy. Our littlest angel, once so connected and typical in every way, was becoming very quickly disconnected from us and from the happy boy he had once been. We could hardly believe our eyes. Our joy was displaced by grief and concern.

Our childhood development books led us to the description of *autism*. In the weeks preceding Parker's 18-month well-baby check, I read every piece of literature I could find on autistic spectrum disorders. At that time, in 1994, the Internet was not yet at my disposal. In addition to the general overview of autism I acquired from books, I turned to local and national autism foundations for information. In the piles of poorly photocopied literature, were words that seemed to jump off of the pages in neon signs – *lifelong, severe, debilitating, pervasive, non-responsive, non-verbal*. This seemed to be more than a childhood illness. Autism was, by my interpretation, a living death sentence. Each descriptive phrase hammered my brain with no less intensity than great physical force. In the cacophony of the horrifying verbiage, I felt numb. Where were the words that we had used to describe him only months ago? Words like *sweet, loving, fun, contented, NORMAL!*

On the day of Parker's 18-month well-baby check in August 1994, I was prepared and educated for the appointment at the office of his new pediatrician (at least I thought I was at the time). I also had decided, beforehand, that I did not want to prejudice the doctor with my fears about Parker. I truly wanted the pediatrician's interpretation of Parker's development. At the end of the exam, he made a note to Parker's medical file that indicated he was well. I spoke up and shared my concerns. He looked at me and asked, "Have you considered that he might be autistic?" He asked this in the same casual way one talks about a car! (Have you ever considered a Chevy or a 4-wheel drive?) "Yes," I retorted. Of course I had. (I had thought of little else for one whole month.) Why had he, I wondered, only minutes earlier, been ready to dismiss Parker from the room with a clean bill of health in hand? He scribbled a name on a note pad. "Call Dr. W (not her real name). She's a developmental specialist at the local hospital. Make an appointment for her to evaluate Parker there."

"Not so fast," I thought. Then I asked, "Do you think his diarrhea and ear infections could be related to his problems? What do you make of the little shaking/shivering episodes he has? Could this all be related? Are there any other specialists he should see?"

"I think you're making too much of this diarrhea thing," he said. "Try cutting back on his intake of juice. And Mrs. Beck, kids get ear infections. We'll switch his antibiotic. Make an appointment at the desk before you leave. Come back in ten days so I can check on his ears."

It took two months to get an appointment with Dr. W, the developmental specialist. During that time, my appetite for more information was insatiable. In the process of researching, I stumbled upon a book that became the beginning of a new way of thinking for me. It was the first book I had read which strongly correlated allergies and behavior, diarrhea and ear infections with specific foods, and physical wellness and nutritional balance with emotional stability. (I have since read dozens more of its kind, which have opened my eyes and my mind to the connection between the gut and the brain, and the gut and general body function.)

After reading the book, we heeded its suggestion to eliminate all dairy products – milk, cheese, whey, casein, etc. – from Parker's diet. Within one week, his ear infections, from which he had suffered for over one year (and which had been resistant to every antibiotic we had tried), disappeared completely and have never returned.

A few more weeks passed, and Dr. W evaluated Parker. A week later, we received her written evaluation in the mail. We were stunned to see in the report that, in her opinion, perhaps Parker had been overly *stressed* by our relocations. She indicated on the report that although I had expressed my concerns about milk and food allergies, she believed those concerns to be of little consequence in Parker's symptoms.

I called her on the telephone to discuss the report, and told her how, in my estimation, the idea of Parker suffering from psychological trauma and stress was out of the question. My children had not been "shuttled" about in any kind of way that would have rendered them traumatized. Gary and I centered our life around our children. They had never even once been left with a babysitter! Even with our relocations, our first priority had always been to unpack their toys and organize their playroom. No, we had been more than conscientious in our care for Parker. Yes, we had moved a few times, but our family life and home environment were as stable as one could possibly imagine. (In retrospect, it was unfortunate to have been put in such a defensive position by her.)

I told her, based upon Parker's physical symptoms, the diarrhea, the shivering episodes, and the changes we had witnessed from dietary modifications, that I felt we should have some other medical testing done as well. In addition, I expressed a strong desire that an EEG and a CAT scan be performed. (My mother had died many years earlier from a brain tumor, as had my uncle. How else could we rule *out* the possibility of physical involvement?) She retorted, "Mrs. Beck, we really need to figure out who we're treating here – *you* or Parker."

Of course, it seemed to me, given the lack of any direction or apparent sincerity and interest on her part, that she wasn't treating *either* of us. I assured her that it didn't matter to me in the least whom she felt she was treating. I wanted certain tests done on Parker, had valid reasons for requesting them, and was quite confident that if she refused to help me, I would find a caring and willing doctor elsewhere. Reluctantly, she referred me to a neurologist at the same hospital.

With that referral, our entrance into the confusing realm of autism officially commenced. A three-hour neurological exam and a CAT scan conjured up words from the medical specialists such as *curious*, and *intriguing*, and phrases such as, *challenging and interesting, but unremarkable*. What is a parent supposed to *do* with those comments? Couldn't anyone utter words like *hopeful, treatable, temporary* and *reversible*? No unfortunately, those words never seemed to come, from anywhere or anyone, and in every case we were sent on our way with little direction and no follow-up.

Parker continued to regress. His behavior worsened, and his chronic diarrhea continued. So did his high-pitched screaming. His gait became erratic and unbalanced. Months passed by and language never appeared. We took Parker to see specialists of every variety. Highly recommended doctors and specialists in New York, Philadelphia and Utah evaluated him.

Allergy tests showed Parker to be allergic to almost everything, yet the pediatric allergist would not say with certainty that the allergies had anything to do with his autistic behaviors. Blood tests revealed nutritional deficiencies of all kinds, and most notably a zinc level that was extremely low. His basal body temperature was always below normal.

EEGs were performed and we were given three conflicting opinions by highly respected professionals and neurologists on whether the tracings were normal or abnormal. There was never any consensus of opinion either about the EEG's or a plan of action or treatment for Parker.

An evoked potential (brain wave) response test was administered on Parker as was a SPECT scan. Both were abnormal, and met two of what we were told were three main indicators for Landau-Kleffner Syndrome, a variant of autism. The SPECT Scan had indicated diminished blood flow to Parker's temporal lobes. The scan showed that his brain was affected bilaterally, with the most significant involvement on the right side. Since his EEG was inconclusive, the "LKS" diagnosis could not be formally made, largely because LKS is classically defined by specific EEG abnormalities.

The doctors in Philadelphia advised us to have a longer, 24-hour EEG done when we arrived back home in Utah. We scheduled the necessary appointment for it, once again, with the staff at our local hospital.

The day of the 24-hour EEG, Parker's head was wired with electrodes as he screamed and writhed in despair. The nurse wrapped his head and bound his hands in gauze to prevent him from tugging at the wires. As the nurse was attending to Parker, a young intern, fresh out of medical school, came into the hospital room and sat down on a chair in the corner. Leaning back, with one leg crossed over his knee, he sat poised and confidently with his clipboard in hand. He looked up at us, authoritatively, over the top of his half-glasses and asked if we had any questions. We had dozens of them — dozens of questions that he, unfortunately, couldn't answer. After we had talked for awhile, I reached for a notepad in my purse on which I had outlined some rough thoughts about Parker's problems and some ideas that seemed worthy of discussion. I even suggested a few treatment protocols regarding diet and allergies. Neither my theories nor my suggestions seemed to interest him. Despite the fact that he had no answers to offer relative to Parker's symptoms and no regard whatsoever for my thoughts, he *was* certain of *one* thing, which he looked up over his glasses long enough to declare. "In these kinds of situations," he said, "miracles just don't happen. So why don't you save yourself a lot of time and stop looking for one? You need to get on with your lives." He was certain of nothing else, but he was certain of that. When the nurse and the intern left the hospital room, I sobbed almost inconsolably. To look at my beautiful son, wired and bound, so unhappy and sick and unable to reach out to me and speak, was emotionally devastating. We should just "get on with our lives." Fancy that.

I had been reading and researching night and day, and using every spare moment between mothering my children, naps, meals, laundry and household chores to talk with doctors and specialists of every kind. I was tired and numb many days, but also realized how important it was to maintain stability for my children and to not allow my fear to invade their world. Gary had been like the rock of Gibraltar, working and traveling, and whenever possible, taking over the child-care responsibilities from me so that I could research. He patiently and lovingly played with them and bathed them at night. He combed their hair while I combed through medical literature.

For days, weeks, and months on end, Gary and I spent our time thinking, worrying, worrying, thinking, crying alone, and crying together, and trying not to do any of it conspicuously in front of our son and daughter, who needed us to be there for them – happy, loving and together.

It is a journey that every parent of an autistic child knows too well. It is a journey that leads us all to more and more questions and so very few answers. It is an experience that no one else can see or feel the way in which we do. The sun comes up every day, and every day within the four walls of the house there lives a very ill child, completely out of control, often very physically sick, and totally unresponsive and incommunicative.

Worse, eligibility for educational and therapeutic services from public schools systems does not take effect until a child has reached the age of three. Many private and appropriate educational programs and therapeutic services are exorbitantly priced, have limited availability, and are financially unfeasible for most families. They are not typically covered by any sort of medical insurance policies.

Gary and I were facing a situation not unlike hundreds of thousands of other families with a child like Parker. We were sent home from almost every expensive and grueling examination and test with no direction and no ongoing assistance from anyone. Family and friends drifted quickly from view, offering little practical support or financial help. Any monetary reserve that we had once had, barely covered the costs of testing and office visits. Our insurance wouldn't cover most of it. Many of these costly tests led to no treatment.

I have always felt that Parker's autistic behaviors were, in a bizarre kind of way, contagious. As we all watched our beautiful little boy crawl into a world of his own, I was also acutely aware of the similar process that was happening in our immediate family.

Entertaining guests quickly became a thing of the past. Even if I had managed to find the moments needed to prepare a special meal or to clean the house and set the table (which is tough when your child is trying to constantly leap from the highest point in your home), I suddenly didn't feel like it. Whom would I invite? Our older friends with no children of their own who had little patience for Parker's behaviors? Not a good choice. How about our younger friends with typical children? An even worse choice. (I found this second group not only frequently intolerant of Parker, but dreadfully painful to be with, in view of our own circumstances.)

Visiting other people's homes was even more out of the question. Taking Parker with us to anyone's home that was not "Parker-proofed" was a nightmare. He would try to destroy everything in sight. Leaving him at home and going without him became an even bigger nightmare because there weren't many willing or able babysitters.

Friends and family members often have NO IDEA about the pain endured by families living with autism. Even simple things become complicated tasks. Meeting at the playground for a morning out is a lonely, hurtful experience. Being the only one who can't stand still in one place, and talk about the wonderfully magical stuff that life and most kids are made of, is emotionally isolating and draining. Having a child affected by autism means having to constantly chase your child so he or she won't run in front of a swing or out into a dangerous street. Having a child affected by autism is not wonderful or magical.

In comparison to emotional concerns, the practical realities of day-to-day life with autistic children are probably the easier part of the equation. The really difficult moments, which occur during the other moments in the day, are the thoughts and the fears that creep into the heart and the brain like insidious invaders who come uninvited and never leave. *"Is this really happening? Maybe it's an allergy: what doctor will listen to me? How can I make time for my other child? Did we do something wrong? Was this the result of his vaccination? What else can I do before it's too late? Where can I get more information? What will I do with the information once I have it? Will this never, ever GO AWAY? What should I be doing that I'm NOT doing? What shouldn't I be doing that I AM doing?"*

For me, it even became increasingly difficult to do things that had nothing directly to do with Parker. I remember picking my daughter up from preschool and waiting outside of the classroom door with the other moms. Their innocent small talk about sibling rivalry or the stresses of everyday life made every jealous hair on my body stand on end. Eventually, I began to get out of my car at the last possible moment just so I wouldn't have to listen to the other moms talk or hear about their day. I wanted *their* day, with all of *their* problems.

The tentacles of autism cleave not only the child, but the family life as well. Each person in the family becomes trapped in autism's clutches. The contagion is slow, painful and debilitating. For even the most optimistic and spiritual people, it is incredibly difficult to believe that this wrenching experience will, in the end, serve some greater purpose.

As our emotional and financial states grew worse (many of his medical tests were very expensive), so did Parker's health and behavior. He refused almost all foods except crackers, french fries and pancakes. We had eliminated all milk products. He vomited any kind of meat or fish. Fruits and juice exacerbated his diarrhea, which was already severe.

Still, the words stared back at me from the autism literature – a *mental* illness? Could a child this young really calculate throwing up a meal? Could he manufacture diarrhea on command? Could he self-induce his red cheeks and runny nose? Could he cause his own sub-normal basal body temperature? What about his practically non-existent blood zinc levels? His toxic levels of certain minerals? His abnormal SPECT scan and Evoked Potential Response tests? His extremely high antibody levels to rubella? A *mental* illness?

For well over six months, we didn't have a network of other parents with which to communicate. While we did ask many professionals to put us in touch with families of children like Parker, patient information was considered confidential. Slowly, we developed a few parent contacts and by asking them for additional referrals, those contacts led to other ones. Our network of patient families soon began to grow exponentially, and so did our understanding of autism.

As Gary and I compared notes, test results and medical reports with other parents whose children had been labeled autistic, we learned that Parker's physiology was not unique. The kinds of physical problems Parker had were shared by an overwhelming number of children whose parents we contacted.

Why was autism classified as a mental disorder and not prominently featured in the medical books as an illness or disease? Furthermore, why had the pediatric, neurological, and psychological experts continually told us that Parker's gastrointestinal problems, nutritional deficiencies and the like had little, if anything to do with his autistic-like behaviors? Did they know that for sure? How?

In February 1995, we moved yet again. This time the move was by choice. We believed, after much investigation that the medical help and educational services for Parker would be better in the New England area. In the dead of winter, in two feet of snow, we moved into our new home. Gary traveled about 50 percent of the time for his job. I unpacked boxes and "held down the fort." Parker remained completely withdrawn and physically ill. There was still no outside help and little sleep. It would take a while to establish ourselves and obtain any treatment and services for Parker. It was a dark and very difficult period in our lives.

The Christmas 1995 season arrived, nearly one year later. Parker had not yet turned three years old. He was still completely non-verbal and his behavior was out of control. He was also still very sick. He would not be eligible for a public school sponsored therapy program until the following month. We had been living in New England for one year and had begun advocating for an educational program, but still none was funded or in place. The physicians and specialists we had contacted in the local area had few treatment options to suggest. We had continued to investigate medical tests and biomedical treatments with other parents and had managed, on our own, to learn about some nutritional and dietary approaches for Parker. Some of these approaches had helped, but they certainly hadn't changed life dramatically for him or for us.

There was not much holiday spirit in my heart, but I tried to plod my way through the tree-decorating and Santa Claus traditions for my daughter's sake. (A tree was anchored to the wall, lest Parker tear it down, and it was decorated from the middle on up, lest he break all of the ornaments.) It was the culmination of a year in which we had tried to address Parker's allergies, diarrhea, and nutrient deficiencies with various anti-fungal medications, powerful antibiotics, and vitamin therapy. We had slaved in the kitchen in order to bake special foods for him, and to concoct mixtures tasty enough to hide the disgusting flavors of the supplements we were trying to get into his system. Some of it helped. Some of it didn't. Some of it he flatly refused. Sometimes it seemed as though we were taking one step forward and two steps back. It was the lowest point in my life emotionally. But things were about to change.

That Christmas Eve, I sat in the kitchen/family room area on the floor, wrapping Parker's gifts. My imagination wandered to the thought of a boy with Parker's same angelic face, who, the next morning, would rush down the steps with his sister, anxious to see what Santa had left. Visions of his smiles as he ripped apart the wrappings filled my head as did the imaginary "oohs" and "aahs" that accompanied his childhood delight.

Thoughts of the harsh reality of autism shattered my momentary illusion, as tears of sorrow and anguish dripped onto the package that lay before me. As I looked down at the box I was wrapping, I thought about how Gary and I had always perceived our children as gifts from God to us. I reflected on how, when Jordan and Parker were handed to me at their birth, each of them was, in my eyes, no less gloriously adorned than the shimmering presents now sitting underneath our Christmas tree. Parker, despite all of his outrageous behavior, and despite all of his physical illness, *was still my gift* from God. But Parker had been stamped, "hopelessly flawed," by specialist after specialist and he was seen by many as a virtual dud in the batch, with an extremely limited warranty at best. Gary and I had been involved and had "bought into" the futile process of trying to find a precise name for his problem (was it autism or PDD or Landau-Kleffner Syndrome?) and a "patch" for it. It was absurd.

To my right, in my kitchen cabinets, were countless bottles of nutritional supplements, strong antibiotics such as Vancomycin, anti-fungals such as Diflucan and Nystatin, DMG, and allergy medications. Adjoining them were bags of organic foods, special breads and fatty-acid supplements. The cabinet was the proverbial "Rubik's Cube" of treatment. We had tried things singularly and in tandem, had seen both improvements and side effects (as had many other children), but Parker was still ill, and we were no closer to identifying the root cause of his illness. It was all so confusing. In a moment of inspiration, looking through this frustrating tableau of assorted supplements and prescription drugs, I realized that all of the things I stared at had one common denominator: they all targeted abnormal intestinal function in some way. Parker's low levels of blood nutrients, his diarrhea, his vomiting, his low zinc, his eating habits, his food preferences, his food allergies – all of it – was intestinally (gut) related. What about his abnormal SPECT scan, his EEG, and his evoked potential? Could the abnormal results on all of those tests be gut-related, too?

Certainly, there were other examples in medicine to substantiate that these things most certainly could be gut-related. After all, doctors at Johns Hopkins had documented great success treating epilepsy with the Ketogenic Diet.[5] One of my doctors had told me of SPECT scans rendered abnormal by food allergies that were corrected by eliminating the offending food. I was not sure about whether the evoked potential results could be related to an abnormal gastrointestinal condition, but my research into this indicated that no one had ever tested such a connection. I considered how many hormones are present in the intestine, and how mentally disoriented an individual can become when hormones like thyroid and serotonin are out of balance. Clearly, a dysfunctional or diseased gut could alter gut hormones and impact behavior. Without digressing to a technical or clinical discussion of these issues, I felt confident that Parker's gastrointestinal problems had been the main cause of his behavioral symptoms all along. The logical question was obvious: "Was autism a behavioral disorder or was autism really a physiological disease, with abnormal behavior and development as byproducts?"

Why were we looking for a patch, a bandage, without trying to heal what might be the actual wound? And what did any of "it" – Parker's physical problems and the contents of my cabinet – have to do with the description of autism? Were his physical problems a byproduct of his behavior? Or, more logically, was it the other way around? Was Parker's behavior a byproduct of his physical problems? Considering that so many other autistic children had the same types of physical problems as Parker, it was clear that no logically-thinking person could believe that the particular physical problems and the behavioral manifestations were not interrelated.

January 1996 brought with it not only the New Year, but also a new *way*. The hit-and-miss, arbitrary, emotionally-wrenching approach to Parker's illness was out. I no longer sought a "patch," I sought to heal the wound. I no longer pondered how Parker fit the definition of autism, I pondered the definition itself. As these simple foundations changed, many other things changed too, especially my energy, my attitude, and me. My goal was to start all over again, to look at the problems before me with a fresh mind, and with a clean slate.

It was a wonderful revelation in the darkness of Parker's autism. I was quickly gaining the right spirit and the right attitude. Now, I needed to start from the bottom up and build a strategic plan that was logical and appropriate to Parker's illness, on which positive actions could be initiated. The right answers demanded the right method.

Chapter Four

Beginning Again: Using the Right Method for the Problem

"Don't try to grow an oak tree in a flowerpot."

~ unknown

It is somewhat of a common annoyance, to those of us who have married into Gary's family, that Gary and his siblings are fairly strong-headed about doing certain things, certain ways. These ways have not simply been born of habit or tradition, but have been, by anyone's account, very well thought out and reasoned, far in advance. These logical approaches to tasks are often annoying to the rest of us, not because they are abnormal or wrong, but because they so often really are, as much as we outsiders hate to admit, *perfect*. Gary, his siblings, and their perfect solutions to life make the rest of us and our approaches to everyday tasks seem so imperfect by comparison.

Somehow, over time, I have come to respect these traits which, in the long run, have made Gary so personally (and perfectly) attractive to me despite the fact that I loathe the burden of having to learn, all over again, the *right* way to do most everything. His ways really *are* better ways, most of the time. Some cases in point: I have learned, when I slice a banana over a bowl of cereal, that my hands never need get messy if I slice the banana while it is still resting on the bottom peel. I have learned how to fold fitted sheets so that they stack neatly in the linen closet. I have learned to load the dishwasher in the most efficient way imaginable and to always put the spoons and forks facing up and the knives facing down. I have learned how to do the laundry and to paint walls, perfectly, and have no doubt that the spouses of Gary's siblings all have as well.

I've also learned the right way, with Gary's help, to build a good fire. Building a good fire never really became an issue until we were several years into our relationship and had a fireplace that would accommodate more than one of those pressed, commercially manufactured logs. After we graduated to a standard sized fireplace, my attempts to create a romantic ambience for the two of us (before autism, when there was time for romance), with lights turned low, soft music, and a fire, were dashed, time and again, by piles of twigs and logs that wouldn't burn or which would require constant attention to keep their flames alive.

One night, Gary took one of my piles of smoldering logs apart, and explained (as I patiently endured the explanation) the correct way to build the fire, starting at the foundation. I was to begin with two dry, split logs placed horizontally and parallel to each other. Then, loosely crumpled paper, and dry kindling were to fill the area under and between the logs. Finally, one more dry split log was supposed to be placed diagonally to straddle the two logs beneath it. The light of one match revealed Gary's fire building method to be flawless. The fire roared for the entire evening, and later, we were even able to add some water-soaked wood to the blaze without diminishing the intensity of the flames. Knowing the right method has since paid off time and again. I can build a fire as well as any Boy Scout.

The history of autism is like a bad fire with sputtering flames and smoldering embers. Theories about autism have been "built" the wrong way. These theories, which have created autism's entire infrastructure, are weak and do not support the kinds of new biomedical information available to us today. Unfortunately, as with building a fire, we cannot compensate for a poor foundation by throwing new evidence and information on the top. All of the paper and all of the kindling, when added on top of a smoldering base, won't create a blaze that endures. At best, it will create minutes of sparks and crackles, and the flames, if any, will not fuel the logs beneath. A foundation poorly built can not create something of integrity or lasting value. Historically, autism's poor theoretical foundation has been poked and prodded to no avail, and more treatments, theories, and philosophies are heaped on top, left to flicker or to die out altogether.

Even those theories and research and treatments having real scientific merit cannot be supported by a community of physicians, educators and researchers who are still fumbling to try to save the smoldering embers below. The cynicism we typically see about emerging potential treatments for autism typically results from this underlying problem. New evidence and real science are often prematurely dismissed in their early stages, as "flash in the pan," "here today, gone tomorrow" nonsense, because *nothing*, even that which contains substance and truth, can or will ever survive atop the faulty, invalid structure on which it has been hoisted.

The destiny of our community, like our children's lives, moves in retrograde motion, in large part because we have accepted a prognosis for an illness that has been based on a false premise, a poor foundation. It is in *changing the premise* of autism that the hopeless desperation of our world begins to take on different form. If we continue to allow autistic spectrum illness to be promoted as incurable, behavioral disorders that carry life sentences for our children, then there are few options left other than to resign ourselves to a life of anger, desperation, fearfulness, resentment, despair, or total complacency. Worse, by such resignation, we renew the license of indifference and impotence to our medical and professional community, and we allow psychologists to define that which actually belongs in the worlds of biology, physiology and science. The cycle and the myth are allowed to continue for another generation. We must re-train our minds and re-educate the medical, educational and psychological professionals. We must change the whole premise of autism if we are to break the cycle and forge new, more hopeful roads.

By changing the premise, we begin to empower ourselves. When we empower ourselves, we change desperation into activation. We turn fear into change. We turn hopelessness and anger into a positive driving force. *We turn the basis for mythology into the basis for science.*

I found that when I changed the premise, everything in my life began to change. In reality, very little had changed, only the premise. By waking up each and every day with the conviction that my son's challenges were a result of biological dysfunction, I was able to handle everything and everyone in a more purposeful and meaningful way. My child was *sick*, not *incurable*. My child was *hurting*, not *hopeless*. My family and I needed *medical help*, not *pity*. My friends and family could assist me if they wished to, and if they did not wish to, or could not find a way, they would have to temporarily be shelved until my son was better. And that would not be forever. The premise changes the mission. The mission changes the actions. The actions change everything.

> **Premise ➡ Mission ➡ Actions**

We must take out all of the faulty logs at the bottom, lay the promising ones aside the hearth, and start over, building our scientific investigation and understanding of autism from the foundation, from the beginning. When we do, our goal needs to reach way beyond that of the low burning embers of past objectives and expectations. Our goal, from the outset, should not be constant management of our flickering fire. Our goal should not merely be well structured, supremely managed *co-existence* with our children, as demanded by the advocates of certain psychological and educational philosophies. Our goal should be the full and lasting success – the *cause* and the *cure*, nothing less. Real science and adequate funding must be the starter logs. Biological origins and an understanding of the physiology in autism must be the paper and the kindling sticks. Behavior management, education, genetic markers, psychology, and all of the rest, will survive and can still thrive at the top. But only biology and physiology can reveal the cause and fuel the cure.

In January 1996, we experienced a rebirth of our intellectual and motivational fire. We cleared out all of the emotional dead wood, we placed the logs still worthy of consideration on the side for a later time, and destroyed the useless kindling and starter logs of hopeless desperation that had been left to dwindle and smolder for way too long.

Parker was clearly physically ill. Had his bizarre behaviors not been part of the equation, had his speech been quite normal, I wholeheartedly believe that the medical community would have paid a lot of attention to his abnormal blood nutrient levels, his chronic diarrhea, his compromised immune response, and a whole host of other things. The medical and psychological obsession with exactly which developmental delay label to attach to him (autism, PDD, LKS, etc.) had overshadowed the physical problems he was experiencing. It seemed, to most of the specialists whom we had consulted, that as long as Parker was autistic (or some variation thereof) all else was not even relevant. A spirit of indifference to the "whole" child abounded; autism was considered a foregone conclusion, dismal and marginally manageable at best.

Parker's illness was clearly more of a disease than those who counseled us were willing to consider. But I resurrected the tag line of an ad once run by United Technologies Corporation, which read,

> *"When forty million people believe in a dumb idea, it's still a dumb idea."*

To this day, it is prominently written in the front of my daily planner. There was no proof that autism was solely a mental disorder. Building a foundation on conjecture for so many decades had been a dumb idea. It mattered little to me that so many people clung to that dumb idea. *I had a son who was destined to lose if I feared being in the minority.*

We felt confident in our rationale; it was based on data from test results and on logic, and we had done much research. Despite the resistance from other schools of opinion, we began to approach Parker's problems in a different way. There was a lot of work ahead, and we were soon to find that there were many more dragons to slay along the way. But slaying those dragons would prove to be far easier armed with the sharpened sword of conviction. Conviction that the premise had been wrong all along – not us.

Since we had already reasoned that his gut was the logical common denominator for all of Parker's problems – physically and behaviorally – we began to research intestinal, digestive, and metabolic diseases. That process led us to a few areas of focus. In order to determine with any certainty what was actually happening inside his gastrointestinal tract, he would need an endoscopy. (An endoscopy is a surgical procedure, done by a gastroenterologist, wherein the patient is sedated and a flexible fiber optic endoscope is advanced through the esophagus to the stomach and the duodenum. The mucosal surface is examined, and biopsies can be taken.) That was no small feat. One does not simply request such a procedure out of curiosity. The issue of requesting to put a child under general anesthesia for an endoscopy was an enormous one to hurdle.

One of the justifications for an endoscopy is to test for celiac disease, an inherited disease in which intolerance to gluten, a protein, causes malabsorption in the intestine and damage to the intestinal lining. Years ago, the *only* way to test for celiac disease was through an endoscopy. In recent years, a blood test to screen for celiac disease – with extremely high accuracy – has been developed. Parker's blood was tested. The results were negative, which nearly eliminated the chance that a doctor would agree to do an endoscopy.

For months, we researched our options, made phone calls, and wrote letters to gastroenterologists in a number of states. In March 1996, a very lengthy, seven-page typed letter that we had written to the Director of Gastroenterology at a hospital in another state (whom I will call Dr. Y) provided the affirmative answer we had sought and prayed for. Based upon a review of Parker's records and the letter we had written, Dr. Y would perform the procedure. We were overjoyed. The date was set for April 18, 1996.

In the interim, we continued to consult with various scientists and specialists about the endoscopic procedure. One researcher (a Ph.D. in biochemistry well known within the autism community) advised us to request two specific tests during the operation. One test was to determine whether anaerobic bacteria were present (a special culture medium could be used to do this during the endoscopy). Another was to test for the presence of yeast and other fungals. He advised us to request these tests because he strongly suspected connections between fungals and bacteria in autism.

There was, in addition to these suggestions, another test in which Gary and I had great interest. During our research, we had read quite a bit on cystic fibrosis (as mentioned earlier, CF had been present in my extended family). Children with cystic fibrosis often have a *Secretin Challenge Test* performed to test their pancreatic function. Not surprisingly, the thick mucus that invades their organs affects their pancreatic function as well. The Secretin Challenge Test can determine pancreatic function and enzyme levels. (Secretin is a hormone that is present in the small intestine. It travels through the bloodstream to the pancreas, where it stimulates the secretion of pancreatic substances, including an abundance of sodium bicarbonate. The presence of the bicarbonate provides an appropriate pH for the action of the pancreatic enzymes.[6])

We believed that this test might also be significant for Parker, based upon his history of digestive problems. We wondered, "Was it reasonable to suspect that Parker's low nutrient levels and diarrhea were due to poor pancreatic enzyme levels or an absence of certain enzymes altogether?" We had already seen his dramatic response to a dairy-free diet. Had he lacked the needed enzymes to digest other foods? Even though we had tried pancreatic enzyme supplementation, wasn't it best to know *for sure* what his actual levels were? The Secretin Challenge Test would provide an opportunity to find out, *and eliminate the guesswork.*

The morning we arrived at the hospital, we spoke with Dr. Y at the elevator doors. Right before Parker was prepped for his procedure, we requested the Secretin Challenge Test. He, and a second gastroenterologist who helped perform the endoscopy, Dr. X (not his real name), agreed to do it.

Following the endoscopic procedure, Gary and I were briefed about the photographic slides that were taken of Parker's intestine. The remaining test results would follow in the next week. We were told that Parker had two main areas of inflammation. These two areas were at the base of his esophagus and the entrance to his duodenum. This inflammation indicated, upon initial impression to the doctors, that there was, for some reason, a problem with acid reflux in Parker's system. We were finally getting a picture of what was actually going on *inside* Parker's body. We hoped that the remaining tests would continue to shed more light.

Chapter Five

The Eclipse:
The End of One Phase and the Dawn of Another

The week following Parker's endoscopy, the hospital lab called us with some preliminary results. The results of the endoscopy and the biopsies were, at first glance, rather unremarkable. So were the cultures for fungals and bacteria. The photographic slides had shown some chronic inflammation, but the biopsies did not indicate celiac disease, or any other identifiable condition. The results of the Secretin Challenge Test had shown Parker's digestive enzymes to be within normal limits, with the exception of lactase, which was deficient.

When all of the endoscopy results had been completed, we were told there was nothing more that Doctors X or Y could do or recommend for us.

Within just days of the endoscopy, however, Parker's bowel movements had suddenly and unexplainably become normal - very normal. His stools not only became formed, but also became dark again, in contrast to the yellowish, foul-smelling stools he had had for two years prior. We noticed an amazing increase in his eye contact with us. So did his therapists, who also knew him well. He was calmer. He slept without a problem all night long. He was happy! Within two weeks after the endoscopy, his language re-appeared for the first time in over two years. His therapist, who had been working rather intensely on getting Parker to receptively identify a small number of flash cards by touching them as she named them, called me downstairs to Parker's therapy room. "Victoria, I think you should come and see this," she said. As the therapist held up each picture of a family member, Parker was saying the name of the person on the card aloud. I was stunned. "Mommy, Daddy, Jordan, Bunny," he uttered, very pleased with himself. "Bunny?, Why is he calling himself Bunny?", we wondered. Then, it clicked. We had frequently called him "Buddy", and this was his version of our nickname for him!

I was so happy I could barely contain myself. Gary rushed home from work, as we spent the next several days walking from room to room with Parker listening to him repeat the words of objects all around the house. The words were not all perfectly articulated, but they were *there*! I had never in my life heard anything that sounded as beautiful as his voice and those words.

By week three, he was saying (still with imperfect articulation) small phrases such as, "I love you," "I want juice," "I want cookie," "Thank you mommy," and "Good-night daddy." He started "dancing" to music and attempting many finger-play songs himself. He began to sing along to his favorite videos. Within weeks, he was completely potty-trained, almost effortlessly. His bowel movements had stayed normal, although his diet had remained the same throughout.

During this entire period of time, we repeatedly called the hospital. Having researched all of the variables before us (anesthesia, diet, therapy, secretin, etc.) we became more and more confident that the secretin Parker had been given had caused these wonderful changes. We were noticing accelerated improvement almost daily. Since Parker was not at that time and had not been on any other supplements, vitamins, or medications of any kind for the previous four months, we knew the physiological changes could not be due to a change in any kind of treatment regimen. His educational program had also not been altered. Parker was receiving about 20 hours per week of one-on-one behavioral therapy.

We compiled letters, theories, and charts on our son's changes, but no one at the hospital believed there could be a connection. One of the charts we composed in 1996 follows:

Summary of Parker's Response to Endoscopy in April 1996

Before Endoscopy	Progress within 3 Weeks After the Endoscopy
Two words	100's of words - will repeat some approximation of any word requested.
No sentences	Short sentences - such as; "I love you," "I want juice," "Good night mommy," "Thank you, daddy."
No flash cards	40 -50 flash cards.

Before Endoscopy	Progress Within 3 Weeks After the Endoscopy
No focus on requested tasks	Will sit and watch carefully. Will perform most tasks after watching once or twice. For instance, will sort by color or category. Will construct more complicated puzzles. Will respond appropriately to "What's this, Parker?"
Diapers only	Completely potty-trained.
Watch Videos	Now, gets "involved" interactively with his videos. He will imitate the hand motions, sing the songs or dance to the music.
Consistent sleeping problems. Although these were much worse when he was 18-24 months, prior to the procedure he was still up numerous times each night.	Has slept through almost every night entirely.
Infrequent (1-2 times/week) "spinning" episodes.	No spinning episodes
Abnormal bowel movements	Normal bowel movements
Excessive water consumption approx. 50 cups per day.	Excessive water consumption - no change approx. 50 cups per day.

Before Endoscopy	Progress within 3 Weeks After the Endoscopy
Limited Diet Preferences (french toast, bananas, french fries, pancakes, crackers, cookies, raisins, chocolate, chicken nuggets).	No Change
No apparent connections made between language and objects.	Many connections made between new language learned and objects. Recites names he has learned on flash cards when he sees the same on computer game or video.
No response to request for gestures	Responds to all kinds of things such as, "Blow a kiss, Parker," "Wave bye bye," "Say bye bye," etc. Will often now spontaneously say these things himself.
No interest in drawing	Cannot keep a pen in sight around the house. Wants to draw constantly. Will draw complete face and name the parts as he draws.
Did not imitate commands	Will imitate almost any multi-step command.
Minimal eye contact	Eye contact 75% of the time.

The gastroenterologists and others repeatedly assured us that the secretin could not be responsible for the remarkable differences.

We began writing letters of inquiry to doctors and other professionals we thought might be able to explain the apparent secretin connection more fully. Gary and I began to document the changes with our home video camera. Though it was difficult to capture the more subtle changes in Parker and his spontaneous language throughout the day, we were able to record significant footage of the incredible metamorphosis that was taking place in our son.

Nearly six months after Parker's endoscopy, we were still sending letters to dozens of researchers, doctors, specialists and scientists in a quest for answers and corroboration for our conviction about the secretin. Finally, in November 1996, one of the doctors with whom we had contact (who was also a parent of an autistic boy) decided to have the same procedure performed on his 6-year-old son. In preparation for this "re-creation," and in an attempt to replicate Parker's procedure *exactly*, I had contacted Dr. X about one month earlier to verify the brand names and doses of the anesthesia and the secretin used on Parker during his endoscopy. Lo and behold, when Parker's medical file was opened to reference the information I was seeking, a new and very significant fact came to light. There, in the doctor's notes, was an indication that Parker had experienced a hypersecretory response to the secretin infusion at the time of his endoscopy. When the secretin had been administered to him, instead of stimulating the normal amount of pancreatic juice, it had stimulated more than five times the normal amount! Despite all of my calls and letters to the hospital regarding the connection between Parker's improvements and secretin, no one had, up to this point, ever communicated this information. Perhaps no one had bothered to look. I don't know for sure.

It was an important piece of information, and it was passed on to the parent of the child awaiting the endoscopy, along with the information on anesthesia and brand names. The date for the second child's endoscopy was set. The same anesthesia and the same dose of secretin were used, but a different gastroenterologist performed the procedure in a different hospital. Significant improvement was noted in this second child after his endoscopy, and his gastroenterologist had observed the same hypersecretory response to the secretin infusion. The secretin connection began to take hold. It had been six months since Parker had received secretin. Now there were two children with similar reactions, and at last, our doctors at the hospital began to take notice.

After the second child showed a response to the secretin infusion, I continued to contact Dr. Y and Dr. X to further discuss the possible benefits of secretin. Dr. X finally became sufficiently interested to explore the connection further.

Gary and I were more than merely excited over these events. The prospect of helping Parker, of helping other children, of being on the verge of real progress made for some optimistic times during these initial weeks. Little did we know, however, that in the midst of such grand promise, other events would occur that would almost eclipse all of these positive events.

In mid-December, 1996, Dr. X performed his first infusion of a child with secretin in an effort to *investigate* the secretin connection (this was actually the *third* autistic child infused). When this third child showed some of the same responses as Parker and the other child, including the hypersecretory response, Dr. X began to explore secretin use in autism more formally. He informed me that he intended to investigate the secretin connection. Needless to say, Gary and I were quite pleased because we were convinced by Parker's stunning turn-around that secretin was a potential treatment for

Parker. What Dr. X did not tell us was that on December 19, 1996, he had filed a disclosure form with the hospital naming himself as the inventor and discoverer of the secretin connection. It would be more than a year later that we would learn of this event.

In the meantime, Gary and I stepped up the pace on our research and efforts. Our focus was to obtain ongoing secretin treatment for Parker and to learn more about secretin so that Parker and others might continue to benefit from its use. Unfortunately, we were told that *other* doctors (in various departments of the hospital) remained skeptical. We were told that these other doctors believed that the changes we had observed in Parker were merely *our* subjective assessments (the key word here is "our"). Because of this, at Dr. X's suggestion (and as part of our ongoing and relentless efforts to convince the hospital to provide secretin treatment for Parker), we made a lengthy videotape showing Parker before and after the endoscopy, during which Parker had received his first secretin infusion. We also arranged for a repeat SPECT scan and a repeat Evoked Potential Test on Parker so that the skeptics could see some totally objective, measurable results. All of this was done for the purpose of obtaining continued secretin treatment for Parker. The tests were quite expensive and required sedating Parker two more times. They also necessitated traveling to a number of other states to have them performed. Although there was only minimal improvement on the Evoked Potential Response Test, the SPECT scan test results were exciting. The SPECT revealed that one half of Parker's brain, which previously had shown diminished blood flow, had now normalized. The videotape we had made of Parker's improvement and the results of the SPECT scan and Evoked Potential Response Test were all submitted to the hospital as part of Parker's medical record. In an additional blood test, we also learned that Parker's extraordinarily high antibody levels to rubella had almost normalized.

In January 1997, the hospital agreed to infuse Parker with secretin for a second time. Following his second infusion, Parker's improvement once again soared. We were encouraged by the positive changes in Parker, and hoped for ongoing treatment. In April 1997, one full year after the original endoscopy, we took Parker back to the hospital for a third infusion. Again, Parker's progression was excellent and we were thrilled. What we did not know or discover until much later was that weeks after this time, in May 1997, Dr. X and the hospital had filed U.S. and foreign patent applications for this new use of secretin as a treatment.

In June 1997, when we were prepared to have Parker infused again, the hospital, without any notice, abruptly terminated Parker's treatment. We were informed that FDA regulations prohibited treatment with secretin, and Parker would not be given any other infusions by the hospital (despite the fact that the hospital was embarking on a formal study of secretin and infusing other patients). Suddenly left on our own, we felt devastated. We felt abandoned by the hospital, especially given that we had brought this discovery to their reluctant and initially unreceptive attention in the first place. More importantly, the hospital made no effort at all to refer us elsewhere, or to assist us with continuity of care for Parker. We finally found care elsewhere, from a compassionate doctor in Utah who had treated Parker in the past.

Our Utah doctor talked with us, listened to us and helped research with us. He sincerely wanted to help Parker and find answers. We were to learn later that, while all of this was happening (as early as May 1997), Dr. X had used the videotape of Parker that we had submitted back in January of 1997. He began to show it, as well as an edited version he had made of it (which included excerpts from the motion picture *Rain Man*), to drug companies, other patient families, media relations representatives and representatives of other large institutions. All of this was done without our knowledge.

Shortly after the hospital abruptly terminated its treatment of Parker, we began to hear stories that Parker's medical records were indeed being used, without our knowledge and for purposes not approved by us. Ironically, we had been trying to obtain Parker's medical records from the hospital ourselves, to no avail. Now, in an effort to learn what was happening, and to regain control of our son's confidential medical records, we again requested a complete copy of Parker's medical records from the hospital. Our repeated attempts to obtain all of the records in Parker's file failed. I even called the Chairman of Pediatrics at the hospital to express my concerns about the use of Parker's confidential medical information and my inability to obtain his records. Even then, the complete set of records was still not sent. We finally obtained several pages from Parker's files in a letter to us, after months and months of trying, but still not all of the records were sent. In a more infuriating development, we continued to get reports from people who said they had been shown the confidential videotape.

In late March 1998, as a last alternative, we hired an attorney to contact the hospital to obtain Parker's medical records and to protect all of his medical information including the videotape. It was at this time, that we first learned that Dr. X had claimed discovery of the secretin connection in December 1996. We soon also learned that he and the hospital had filed patent applications in the United States and abroad in May 1997. We further discovered that the videotape of our son had been used in presentations to pharmaceutical companies and others as early as May 1997. It was almost inconceivable to us that in seeking help and treatment for our son, our own discovery and hard work were now being used in these ways. Even more disturbing to us was learning that Parker was being used by the hospital as a "poster child" of sorts for secretin use in autism during the same period of time we were unable to get the hospital to administer or treat Parker with secretin.

Our attorney discussed these matters with the representatives of the hospital, specifically regarding the conduct of its employees, agents and representatives. In July 1998, the hospital's legal counsel and a representative for academic research flew to meet with our legal counsel and us. We presented to them substantial and clear documentation including piles of correspondence, phone records and research to substantiate all of the events described above. Within a short time, the hospital representatives concluded that I was the original discoverer of the secretin connection and that the patent rights rightfully belonged to me. The hospital assigned those rights and inventorship to me. They also provided the complete medical records we had been requesting – the medical records that had prompted the involvement of our attorney in the first place.

We had engaged our legal counsel primarily to secure Parker's medical records. At the outset, we had no idea what else we would uncover along the way. As the other issues became evident, we chose to investigate those as well, not for personal or financial gain, but out of principle. As the quote at the top of this chapter says, "It is important that people know what you stand for, but equally important that they know what you won't stand for."

In July 1998, we assumed that the issues with the hospital were resolved. We chose not to publicize these matters within the autism community, or publicly in any way, because we saw no positive purpose in doing so. Around the same period of time, several major newspapers and well-known television programs caught wind of the secretin phenomenon. Several dozen children had by then been infused with secretin. Many of their parents and doctors were reporting terrific results. We were contacted by news crews about our discovery, and were subsequently interviewed. Not too surprisingly, the media was very interested in the more melodramatic elements of our story. We wanted the emphasis to remain on the potential hope that secretin and further biological research held for the treatment of autism, not the other events that had transpired.

We remained fairly silent about many of the more distasteful aspects of our experience, because our primary interest was always to help Parker and other children like him obtain treatment. Despite our intentions to move forward in a positive light, we were frustrated by a number of events, including gossip that claimed we had sued the hospital and Parker's doctors (which we had not). We also received a disturbing phone call in October 1998, from Dr. X's wife after *Good Morning America* and *Dateline NBC* had aired stories about children who had responded to secretin. She had gained access to our personal and unlisted private phone number that was listed in Parker's confidential medical files at the hospital. The hospital and its legal counsel were made aware of the call, but still, we chose to exercise restraint.

From the educational and psychological communities came all kinds of criticisms. There were criticisms about secretin treatment and its "off-label" use (never mind the fact that since there are no approved treatments for autism, many other drugs – frequently used on autistic patients – were technically "off-label" as well). There were criticisms of the open-minded doctors who administered secretin to their autistic patients. There were rumors (the truthfulness of which were *never* substantiated or investigated) that parents were buying secretin on the black market and were mortgaging their homes to purchase it for their children. Ironically, some of the professionals who were calling for clinical trials were quick to accept these negative rumors about secretin as being true but were skeptical about the hundreds of success stories being related by intelligent parents and doctors about secretin treatment. These same professionals were casting doubt on the positive improvements reported by parents, yet were willing to believe the negative rumors at face value.

There were also criticisms of Gary and me from people who tried to cast aspersions on our motives and involvement with secretin. The more desperate the critic, the more irrational and more pitiful the attack. The criticisms were not based in fact, but emanated, in my judgement, from a profound insecurity that somehow, a potential medical treatment for at least one subgroup of children with autism threatened the importance of other medical agendas and other types of therapy and education. Such outcries were as unreasonable then as they are now. There was still much to be studied. Gary and I were proponents of strong behaviorally-based educational programs and had been quite vocal about the role of Parker's education in his tremendous progress. No logically-minded persons, especially us, had ever implied that secretin was a "magic bullet," a "one size fits all" approach to autism. Ironically, the secretin-autism connection was sensationalized primarily by people who wanted desperately to make it seem unrealistic. By so doing, they made secretin treatment much easier to dismiss.

We were told of one school for autistic children that criticized secretin as a "craze" and strongly discouraged parents from seeking secretin treatment for their children. Why should anyone believe that both an educational regimen and a biomedical treatment couldn't co-exist in a complementary manner? In fact, in what other disease do we deny the importance of appropriate and ongoing therapies or education? Why do the proponents of certain educational approaches deny the potential for the medical treatment of children whose clinical profiles *clearly* indicate a disease process?

The purpose of relating the secretin story and sharing the facts that preceded it is not, and has never been, to urge parents to try secretin or to espouse any one medical treatment in particular. Out of our story comes something more intrinsic to the fates and futures of our children than merely one biomedical approach to this horrible affliction called autism.

The hurdles before our ill children, and us, are many and diverse. Because autism has been defined historically as it has, the abnormal physiology of our children (with the exception of the brain) has been largely ignored. In addition, the politics of our medical community, and the politics within the autism community itself, make it nearly impossible to chart a path of progress and to reverse the futility of patterns that are so deeply ingrained and familiar. *The secretin story is a sad and disturbing testament to all of this.*

As parents facing the realities of this severe illness each and every day, our surrender to the foundation of failure before us is often so slow and insidious that it becomes imperceptible. Our children's challenges can be so overwhelming that our remaining resolve to individually enact monumental change within these systems seems far beyond our capacity. In Part II of this book, we discuss an approach to these problems – a plan of empowerment – but for now, suffice it to say that *it is our individual empowerment that will ultimately shape a different destiny for our children.* We must not think of empowerment as trying to fuel a fire that has heretofore proven itself to be incapable of providing the cure for autism. We must think of our empowerment as lighting a match to the kindling of a new fire altogether, on top of which some of the old logs may be fueled and in which some of the sodden wood of our past can not be allowed. That lighted match of empowerment must start with wisdom, and find its strength in truth and conviction. It must be kept safe, from the strong winds of habitual resistance and the politics of the past and the present.

Chapter Six

Autism Research:
The Black Hole of Truth or a Beacon of Hope?

"The vast majority of human beings dislike and even actually dread all notions with which they are not familiar... hence innovators have generally been persecuted, and always derided as fools and madmen."

~ Aldous Huxley

While Parker's experience with secretin treatment has been enormously successful, Gary and I have steadfastly avoided ever persuading others to try secretin treatment. We have shared our story, but recognize that secretin may not be effective for every autistic child. More importantly, we respect every parent's right to determine appropriate intervention for his or her own child. *Let it be perfectly clear at the outset of this chapter, that the purpose of this chapter is not to debate the use of secretin or to compel any other parent to seek secretin treatment for their child.* The purpose of this chapter is much, much broader and more fundamental.

Because we, as parents, are indeed ultimately responsible for the care and treatment of our children, we depend upon the truth and accuracy of the information we receive from the medical, scientific, psychological, pharmaceutical and educational communities. What then, do we do if that information is not correct? More importantly, *why* would such information *not* be correct? The answers to these questions are not simple ones.

In his book entitled, *Vaccination, Social Violence and Criminality*, Harris Coulter states,

> *"Power corrupts in medicine as elsewhere. In granting absolute power to medical organizations we have made them candidates for absolute corruption."*[7]

Coulter is referring here to the vaccination strategy of today's medical and pharmaceutical industries. But we need not even digress to the subject of vaccine policy to find other examples that directly affect us within the autism community.

As I write this book, I am aware of dozens of studies being carried out to investigate the effects of secretin use in autism. Some of the early studies were rushed to the forefront, quickly commenced, quite possibly, by intense interest from within the parent community. This is an important factor to highlight from the outset. When researchers or doctors feel pressured by their patients, the studies that result may be initiated not due to legitimate scientific interest, but in response to unwelcome patient pressure. Arguably, this could result in a negative bias in some cases.

The biases of the research community can greatly determine the outcome of laboratory studies. Even in double blind, placebo controlled trials, failure can be ensured in several ways. One of these ways is to use measures of outcome that are irrelevant to treatment.

In one study, secretin was administered to an autistic patient population including children with seizure disorders. Secretin and a placebo were administered to each of the patients in the study, on separate occasions, and the behavioral changes of the patients were measured after secretin and placebo, using a frequently used diagnostic instrument. The study concluded that there was no difference between the results from infusions of secretin and the placebo.

Weeks after this study was completed, I began to receive a barrage of letters, phone calls and emails from the parents of the patients in the study. These parents expressed their surprise and dismay that the study had reported no responses to secretin.[8] One mother wrote that she had clearly documented "better sleep, better concentration and more initiation of appropriate play" in her child after infusion.[9] Another posted about a child who had "amazing results," whose therapists, teachers, and family saw huge results with the secretin and huge regressions after discontinuing it.[10] I learned of still another mother who reported that her child "just soared" after getting the secretin. The improvement was noted and commented on by many people, including the assistants in the doctor's office, yet according to the mother, the doctor heading up the study said the mother was the victim of wishful thinking.

Another mom wrote to me to say that she was receiving ongoing prescriptions for secretin with "no hassle" from the doctor who conducted the study.[11] (Odd, I thought, from a doctor claiming to have determined no positive results.)

Another parent posted her sentiments to an autism Internet discussion group. She stated that the particular doctor had promoted some conventional drug treatments and had gotten upset with the mom when she raised the issues of their side effects. She felt he was not open to the possibilities of secretin use before he knew for sure either way.[12]

And still more feedback from another mom, who for some reason, felt that the doctor was out to disprove secretin, adding that she didn't think he believed in the "gut issues" in autism.[13]

A separate research team designed a secretin study on patients ranging considerably in age. The patients received a *single* dose of secretin (in this case, experimental synthetic secretin not yet claimed or proved to be effective in autism) *or* placebo, after which results were measured utilizing standard behavioral assessments. Once again, no compelling differences were noted between the secretin group and the placebo group of patients.

In both of these studies, the authors stated that they had performed double blind, placebo controlled trials. While that may be true, was the treatment outcome measurement relevant to the treatment? Can we ever expect to fairly evaluate the effectiveness of secretin or any other biomedical intervention in autism if we do so using general diagnostic assessments? *Can any study, for any biomedical intervention, be predestined for failure if an assessment tool never intended or designed to measure change in response to treatment is used?*

In the *Handbook of Autism & PDD – 2nd Edition*, edited by Donald J. Cohen and Fred Volkmar, chapter 21, "Diagnostic Instruments in Autism Spectrum Disorders," Catherine Lord comments on the types of behavioral assessments used in both of the above studies:

> "Often, investigators have attempted to use diagnostic instruments to measure change in response to treatment. On the whole, this approach has not been very successful. In part, success has been lacking because most diagnostic instruments were designed to include a wide range of deficits associated with autism and *are not sufficiently sensitive to changes within an individual.*"[14]

Would we expect to measure the effectiveness of insulin (another familiar hormone) on a diabetic patient by designing a study in which patients were given *one dose* of insulin and later assessed as to their *apparent* fatigue or appetite? Would we have *no* interest in measuring, at the very least, their blood sugar?

The effects of potential *biological* interventions for our autistic children are often measured by diagnostic instruments, which are, in response to treatment, "not sufficiently sensitive to changes within an individual." In addition, in the case of secretin, a mere single dose is sometimes being used.

(Are we to believe that researchers would measure, in the same way, the effectiveness of psychoactive drugs they readily prescribed to our autistic children? Would they use a single dose, in patients who may or may not be taking other prescription medications, such as corticosteroids and anticonvulsants, concurrently? Is it quite possible, where secretin is concerned, that these agents may block secretin's effects or even interact negatively? How can the efficacy of secretin be measured with a single dose in the presence of confounding variables such as the ones mentioned? Furthermore, are we to believe for a moment that doctors would test other frequently used interventions, such as anticonvulsants or steroids, after one dose, using behavioral assessments intended for *diagnostic* purposes?)

We need to examine the ways in which our researchers may be approaching the whole issue of biology in autism. We will never uncover the biological causes of autism without a willingness on the part of more researchers to investigate physiological endpoints of treatments such as secretin. We will also never really get to the truth in research if the tools we use to evaluate behavioral changes are inappropriate.

If the medical community wants to investigate the merits of secretin treatment in light of the hundreds of success stories shared by intelligent and knowledgeable parents and doctors, wouldn't it be prudent to investigate the answers to some of the following questions?

Does endogenous secretin-release function properly in the guts of autistic children? (When stimulated with hydrochloric acid during endoscopy, do children with autism release secretin to the same degree as normal controls?)

Does secretin somehow affect serotonin levels, triggering the brain in a particular way?

Do brain scans show a specific response to secretin infusion?

What is the effect of secretin on EEG activity?

Does secretin treatment affect abnormal urinary peptide levels in children where such levels have been measured to be high?

Does secretin affect immune response or histamine levels?

Does secretin alter thyroid function? (Could that explain the rises in basal body temperature documented in some children?)

Are the effects of secretin, like insulin, dose dependent? (Would we test the effects of thyroid, testosterone, or estrogen by giving a single, very high dose?)

There are more questions, which have not been fully revealed about some secretin studies but which need to be taken into consideration in future studies:

Are the children in the study being treated concurrently with other drugs?

Is it possible that some drugs (such as valproic acid, steroids, antibiotics or antifungal medications) could interfere with secretin response? (How do we know for sure?)

Are the children on special diets? Would a gluten-free or casein-free diet be more likely to produce a positive response to infusion?

Because secretin is an intestinal hormone, would fasting before infusion be more likely to produce a positive result?

Unfortunately, we may never know the answers to these questions and others, because:

♦ Some of the initial researchers didn't look, or ask, or take the necessary steps to investigate.

♦ Behavioral assessments (not intended to measure treatment outcome) after a *single secretin infusion* didn't yield positive results, discouraging further investigation by other scientists and doctors.

♦ Certain physicians, psychologists, and educators have built their entire reputations, practices, and livelihoods in the autism community. When we seek to change the premise of autism, we are changing the perception and the value of the practices of many professionals in the process. Investigating the *biology* of autism and the *physiology* taking place with certain treatments is threatening to many people for many reasons.

Fortunately, there is promise and hope in the balance. Many determined parents and dozens of medical professionals have not been deterred by studies that have overlooked the physiology of secretin. Preliminary results are encouraging and exciting. Some doctors and parents have documented clear changes in opioid peptide levels after secretin infusion. Others have noted changes in visual perception, normalization of basal body temperatures, histamine levels and gastrointestinal function.

The reports of positive behavioral changes are too numerous to mention in great detail, but the surveys of parents and doctors alike indicate profound changes in the behavioral symptoms of children infused with secretin. Some of these changes did not occur until three or four infusions.[15] The surveys from dozens of highly-respected doctors and parents worldwide have indicated remarkable results.

Our personal files and the files of doctors and researchers are packed with communications from parents who have reported incredible secretin success stories – of children speaking their first words after infusion, paying attention in a classroom environment for the first time, and becoming potty trained shortly after secretin treatment. Many of these changes are documented clearly on videotapes and on surveys by therapists, teachers, physicians and parents.

Are all of these parents and doctors *deluded*? Are hundreds of reports of improvement all *fiction*? Have hundreds of parents *imagined* such things as the disappearance of chronic diarrhea, the atypical hypersecretory response measured during endoscopy, the normalization of basal body temperatures, and the onset of normal sleep patterns after secretin infusion? The parents and doctors I know who have reported these dramatic secretin responses have been quite level-headed and intelligent.

Is it just possible that some of the studies that were rushed to the forefront neglected to consider any *physiological* measures of outcome (such as the aforementioned ones) and used behavioral assessments not effective in measuring treatment outcomes?

We must take a closer look at the way research is being carried out regarding the biological causes of autism and the biomedical treatments for it. In general (and not exclusively with regard to secretin), we must not be misled by what may be mislabeled science. *We must not only pay close attention to how autism has been defined, we must pay close attention to how science is being defined as well.* Many within our research community are quick to point toward the unreliability of human observation. If only some of these same individuals would be as eager to inspect the fallibility of the scientific method when it is poorly or inappropriately applied. Clinical trials, placebo controls, and laboratory settings do not, in and of themselves, constitute science, especially if they are ill-conceived from the outset.

We must also look at another important component in the process of finding answers for our children – *wisdom*. Do our researchers, scientists and psychologists exercise wisdom in this journey? Do we, as parents?

What exactly is wisdom? Is it knowledge? Is it experience? Is it rational, empirical study? Or, is it something much, much more?

How important is wisdom in the scientific realm and how does it impact the autism community at large? Do our scientists need to possess wisdom *in addition to science? Is science absent wisdom really science at all?*

Chapter Seven

More Than a Mere Spark of Light: Wisdom for All

"Wisdom is not wisdom when it is derived from books alone."

~ Horace

Our present-day understanding of the word wisdom is "being wise" or "possessing knowledge."[16] When we look back at the Biblical interpretation of the word, we find something quite different.

The word "wisdom," as it was used in the Old Testament, referred to the academics and the scholars in royal courts on the one hand, and was also used to describe goldsmiths, midwives, architects and musicians on the other. Wisdom was in part "knowledge, intellect and skill" and in part "spirituality, goodness, kindness, and purpose to other men and society."[17]

It is in the intersection of these two facets of wisdom that important considerations are revealed. True wisdom is not simply "possessing knowledge" as we commonly think of the term. Wisdom, actually comprised components of the *mind* and of the *heart*. These components contained qualities and virtues necessary to transcend the world of the mediocre and to enter the domain of the truly wise. Put into graphical terms, wisdom might look like this:

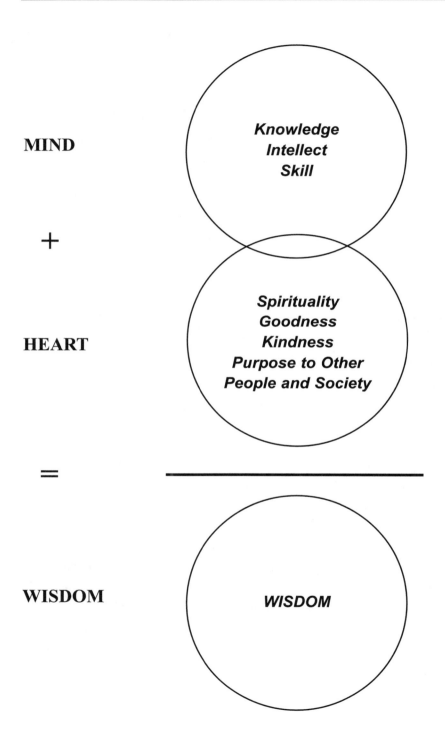

MIND

Knowledge
Intellect
Skill

+

HEART

Spirituality
Goodness
Kindness
Purpose to Other
People and Society

=

WISDOM

WISDOM

Clearly, as parents, we share equally with the scientists and the academics in our capacity for wisdom. The medical and scientific communities should welcome the wisdom we have to offer with a humble and open spirit. After all, the information we have to offer about our own children and the observations that we report regarding their behaviors, improvements, and daily living patterns, *are* valuable. In fact, they are every bit as valuable, (and perhaps *more* reliable) as information garnered by a clinical psychologist in an evaluation, information gathered by a scientist in a clinical laboratory setting, or information assessed by a physician in a physical exam. We have the most complete frame of reference on our children. We know them, *fully*. We must never, ever, underestimate the value of our "gut feelings," our parental intuition, and our heartfelt notions about our children. Wisdom is not one-dimensional, and we must never allow our capacity to exercise our parental wisdom and to shape our children's destinies to be diminished. Wisdom is not the exclusive domain of the Ph.D.'s, the M.D.'s and the academics. It is not *solely* about rational knowledge, clinical trials, and superior degrees.

Certainly, this is not to discourage the pursuit of academic knowledge or the belief in sound medical/scientific studies and methods. Traditional medicine has offered us countless and invaluable breakthroughs. There is no denying that modern medical advances immeasurably enhance our lives. *But as we shift into a new era of bringing autism into the laboratory, we must make sure that the scientific minds behind the science are not operating without balance – without wisdom.* The scientific mind, and heart, must be open and unprejudiced. If from the outset, the scientist or researcher is wholly concentrated on preserving or promoting a particular agenda or theory, or if the scientist or researcher is wholly concentrated or emotionally predisposed to disproving a theory, then our children's well being will not be served.

In 1923, Ernest H. Starling (one of the co-discoverers of the secretin hormone in 1902) delivered an address known as the Harveian Oration to The Royal College of Physicians of London. It was entitled "The Wisdom of the Body."

Starling hailed William Harvey (who, in 1628, three centuries before Starling spoke of him, discovered the circulation of the blood) as his "colleague in spirit" and reflected upon the revolution in medicine that had been sparked by Harvey's work.

> *"...he (Harvey) probably failed to appreciate the extent of the dark shadows cast by the great clouds of ignorance which still had to be dispersed."* [18]

He went on,

> *"For countless ages, mankind had learned slowly and painfully by experience. The more observant had, from time-to-time noticed certain recurring sequences in the infinity of fortuitous phenomena continually presented to them, and as a result, man had by slow degrees improved his lot and his powers over the forces of nature."* [19]

Starling urged others, not only scientists and physicians to search out "the secrets of nature" and said,

> *"This implies that we are to give free scope to the spirit of curiosity, with some measure of which **every man**, is endowed. We ourselves are but part of the order of nature, and **all** knowledge therefore is contributory to the science of medicine."* [20]

He concluded his talk and incorporated this passage from the Book of Job:

"Who hath put wisdom in the inward parts? or who hath given understanding to the heart?"

Surely, Starling was fascinated with the intricacies and the awesome choreography of the human body. He had a deep reverence for the manner in which our physical organisms were so perfectly knit. His profound respect for William Harvey's "understanding of the heart" was clearly communicated throughout Starling's oration. But Ernest Starling's challenge to attain a comprehension of "the wisdom of the body and understanding of the heart" is a call to *every* individual to exercise their God-given wisdom when trying to *understand* the *physical* intricacies of the body.

As parents, our observations and assessments are often presumed by others to be unscientific, emotionally driven and tainted, anecdotal and subjective at best. Starling's words remind us and assure us that we *are* endowed with not only the curiosity to seek out the secrets of our children's autism, but the knowledge, ability and wisdom to contribute to their ultimate cure.

It is also relevant to point to the tales of *emotionally driven and tainted responses* from within the medical, psychological and scientific community about particular autism theories or interventions. Our professions, even if they are in medicine and research, obviously do not *shield* us from our own humanity. Neither should they *deny* the wisdom of our own humanity or the humanity of others.

In our search for the truth, in our quest for *real science* and *meaningful data*, we must also seek wisdom, and reject emotionally driven, narrow and rigid agendas. We all should seek the humble and open mind. *All* of us. Wisdom, not merely empirical thought or technical expertise, will steer the course of truth in research and empowerment within the autism community at large.

Our wisdom leads to our empowerment. Our empowerment will lead to positive, progressive change. Our empowerment is the light that will transcend the darkness of autism. It is the product of our wisdom and our positive energy. *Our empowerment is the aurora on the dark side of Venus.*

Part II

Chapter Eight

The Aurora on the Dark Side of Venus:
An Introduction to the Plan of Empowerment

"Adversity can set me helpless on my back,
but she cannot keep me there;
nor can four walls limit my vision."

~ adapted from Margaret Fairless Barber

The hopelessness of autism is rooted in and fueled by a premise that is invalid and scientifically irresponsible. It asserts that autism is a lifelong, behavioral disorder and does not even acknowledge the physiological dysregulation of many autistic individuals. The invalid premise itself is at the very heart of our inability to find the cause and the cure for autism. The invalid premise is the ball and chain around our wrists and ankles and minds and souls. It defies wisdom and it defies reality. Useful biomedical interventions have restored many children to high functioning lives and even to recovery.

To merely say that we *shouldn't* accept the invalid premise regarding autism is not enough. We need to examine why we *have* accepted it in the past. We are a community that has been weakened by more than the prognosis we are told is inherent in our children's labels. Many of our children do not sleep normally or act normally. They do not eat normally or speak normally. Even the most routine daily events are huge challenges because our children do not easily comply and often do not attend to our wishes or our presence in any kind of socially accepted way. The duties of everyday life are so overwhelming that we often cannot find the strength to fight the systems and institutions that have promoted the myths we need to defy. We need services, we need biomedical research, we need answers, we need help and we need hope. But, ironically, the condition itself, with its trappings and its contagion to every aspect of our lives, isolates us and often renders us weakened and exhausted.

We are in a place we never intended to be, with no clear-cut indication of how we arrived, isolated in large measure by the uniqueness of the condition that put us there, and with few tools, people or direction to assist us in finding our way out. The label that has been attached to the name of this foreign place is inadequate and ill-defined. What's worse is that we have been cast off to survive with a map that leads nowhere and a navigation guide that is ambiguous, antiquated, unreliable, and assumes no cure is possible. From where we stand, every road in every direction appears cloud-covered, uncertain and obstructed. We are, metaphorically, on "Venus," feeling desperate, weakened and powerless, individually and as a community, against the forces all around us. Our life, like Venus, moves in retrograde motion primarily because the premise of autism is counter-productive, and does not propel us in the direction of answers. Our children are often out of control and helpless. Are we out of control and helpless along with them?

By December 1995, autism had eaten away the very depth of my soul, and the hollowness of it screamed back at me in a way I had never heard before. In my desperation, I had become weak. In my willingness to subscribe to a myth, I had betrayed my own sense of logic and wisdom. My sense of value and power in my son's life seemed diminished by the systems surrounding me.

Then, a very simple thing occurred to me. I felt weakened *because* of the premise. I felt desperate *because* of the premise. I felt fearful *because* of the premise. I was powerless *because* of the premise.

Everything could change if I first changed the premise. So I did. Parker clearly had medical problems. Every blood nutrient test we had ever run on him was abnormal. Same for allergy testing. Same for hair analysis, urine analysis and fungals. His SPECT scan showed diminished blood flow. His evoked potential response tests had shown an abnormal response. His antibody levels to mumps and rubella were sky high. He had chronic diarrhea. My thought process went something like this:

> *The origins of Parker's problems weren't psychological, they were **physiological**.*

If Parker's problems were physiological ones of unexplained origin, then how could anyone say with assurance that his condition was lifelong and that he was incurable?

> *Parker's physiological problems weren't incurable, just inadequately explored and explained.*

If Parker's problems weren't psychological or incurable, the label of autism referred only to the *byproduct* of his underlying condition, which had no name yet. That was the beginning of a new life for Parker and for me. It began with a new premise, which I plastered in the front of my mind and my planner.

> *"Parker is a health-impaired child, suffering from inadequately explored and potentially curable physiological problems which have caused his behavioral manifestations."*

I have since refined my original thoughts and premise, but the essence of this new premise has always remained intact. Changing the premise changed my attitude, my actions, my perseverance, my decisions, my relationship with doctors and with specialists. It even changed my relationship with my family and friends. I was not on a sinking ship or a piece of driftwood, I was on a voyage and I needed a powerful boat to ride the waves! Those who wanted to help me navigate were welcome. However, those who didn't wish to make the journey with me weren't going to stand in my way.

The tools that I once had had at my disposal were few and useless. The old tools were meaningless labels and roadmaps that led nowhere. Changing the premise had broadened the tools at hand. My own wisdom and empowerment were central to the voyage because now the quest was hopeful. Abandoning the myth of hopelessness, I left the confines of fear and desperation behind as well. Changing the premise revealed my faith and made me stronger. Most importantly, changing the premise accurately depicted what was wrong with Parker. I could look at the problems before me with clarity of purpose and a commitment to action.

Of course, it was abundantly clear that I was still on "Venus." Parker was still destroying the house, sleeping erratically, non-verbal, non-responsive, uncooperative, and generally "zoned out." But now, I could see the aurora emerging in the distance and in its presence, I no longer felt trapped.

It was our empowerment that was the aurora on Venus. It was this emerging plan of empowerment that eventually allowed me to fully understand my role in my life with Parker, and to become actively involved in the direction of his health care and the process of his ongoing recovery. It was this plan of empowerment that ultimately resulted in the discovery of secretin treatment in autism. *A simple plan, a meaningful plan of action.*

Along the way, we encountered many roadblocks, endured a fair amount of criticism, experienced the politics of medicine in full swing, witnessed the cruelty and ignorance of others as never before, and worked harder and slept less than at any other time in our lives. It was not been an easy road. Yet it was a hopeful one. Hopeful because, despite the turbulence, empowerment kept our personal focus on the goal. For every negative encounter, there were more positive ones that somehow always triumphed. For every individual who tried to make our ship (our mission) run aground, there were more individuals who came aboard and helped us steady our course. A major shift occurred in *who* was involved in the process. As we refused to tolerate the "business as usual" approach to Parker's illness, the old guard of autism was replaced with a progressive new team. The new team had fresh and insightful thinking and bright, rational, new ideas. The new team had doctors, scientists, and researchers who thought "outside the box." The new team was not inextricably linked to one particular ideology. The new team cared, really cared, about my child, my family, and me, and exercised respect every step of the way. There was a "law of attraction" to the empowerment process. When we approached autism with a revolutionary attitude, a revolution began to take place.

In particular, a few memories stand out in my mind. There was the call to Dr. Rimland after Parker had been refused further secretin treatment by the hospital. Within hours, he had hooked me up with Dr. David Gregg, a retired California scientist who spent days and nights with me on the phone doing research, helping me, and explaining the molecular structure and pathways of secretin in terms that I could understand.

There was a call to Dan Bourque, a local attorney, whom I didn't know and had never met. We had been trying to obtain Parker's medical records for months to no avail, and didn't know where to turn next. We didn't have the financial resources to retain an expensive lawyer, but knew we had gone as far as we could go on our own. We needed help. With compassion for a total stranger with an autistic child, Dan volunteered to intervene to try to get the medical records for us.

There were calls that poured in after the *Dateline NBC* piece aired, from doctors across the country (and beyond) who wanted to know, "How can I help these children?" They were the answers to the prayers of parents who had asked, "How can I find a doctor who will listen?" New doctors, *forward-thinking doctors, caring, compassionate, intelligent, rational doctors.* Doctors, the vast majority of whom, contrary to sensationalized and largely unsubstantiated media reports, never tried to overcharge parents or prey upon the autism community, but who truly tried to help their patient families, sometimes at close to no profit whatsoever.

There were, and still are, parent stories too numerous to relate that are a testament to the strength within our community. Parents such as Ricci Hedequist and Eric Einbinder, initiated Internet autism discussion groups in an effort to raise the level of integrity of parent interactions with one another and to foster healthy parent-professional relationships. Parents such as Rick Rollens and Shelly Reynolds, became instrumental in raising funds for autism research and advocating for scientific scrutiny of the potential connections between childhood vaccines and autism. Parents standing up for what is right. *Forward-thinking, caring, compassionate, intelligent, rational, determined parents.*

The process of empowerment is challenging, yet promising. In it, we find that human kindness, wisdom and goodness abound. *We need no longer settle or strive for anything less.*

It has been three and a half years since Gary and I developed our plan of empowerment. It has changed the course of Parker's life and the destiny of our family. In sharing our plan, it is our hope that others will find new hope, new meaning, new joy and the truth about the nature of their child's illness. Briefly stated, here are the eight steps to our plan. The following chapters discuss each step in more detail.

- ◆ I will adopt a new, more accurate premise for the term "autism," which is purposeful and hopeful, which correlates to my child's unique medical history and behavioral symptoms, and which propels me into positive and meaningful action on my child's behalf.

- ◆ In order to chart an effective roadmap for my child's recovery, I will identify the specific educational, therapeutic, and medical interventions which may be appropriate for my child in each six-to-nine-month interval. I will also identify the ways to make those interventions happen.

- ◆ I will implement a system of empowering beliefs about my child's illness, and about autism in general, that is forward-thinking and useful to my child, my purpose and my actions.

- ◆ As much as possible, I will eliminate the little stresses in my life that can potentially add to the larger stresses. I will try to employ the "Six Stress Savers" in my interactions with others!

- ◆ After love and prayer, knowledge and wisdom used together are the two most powerful tools I have to help my child recover.

- ◆ I will build upon my foundation of facilitation partners, network with them regularly and will keep records of positive interventions and strategies that may relate to my child or my family.

♦ Only meaningful questions will be permitted in my daily journey with my child. I will encourage the same from those around me, including family members and specialists, because these questions will ultimately determine the answers I will find.

♦ I will never deny my God-given, intuitive sense as a parent, and I will be confident in my observations and assessments of my own child. Furthermore, I will always look for the light (the connections and the clues) from within my child to help direct the course of his recovery.

The eight steps of our plan are a unique blend of the pragmatic with the pervading philosophy of this book. Autism is to be fought with mind, body and soul. Our children are depending on us.

Some of the steps have common themes; consequently there are some redundancies within them. Such repetition can be a *good* thing (literary standards against redundancy notwithstanding). We can perfect our response to our situation through such repetition, in much the same way as we learn a musical instrument or learn to swing a golf club properly. We can learn to think a different way using organized methodology, just as we teach our challenged children using organized step-by-step teaching methods.

We are a community that shares similar problems, but we will be a stronger community if, along the road we travel, we can share our solutions to those problems, too.

Chapter Nine

Empowerment Plan Step #1:
Adopting a New Premise

*"There are no such things as incurables,
there are only things for which man has not found a cure."*

~ Bernard Baruch

> **I will adopt a new, more accurate premise for the term "autism," which is purposeful and hopeful, which correlates to my child's unique medical history and behavioral symptoms, and which propels me into positve and meaningful action on my child's behalf.**

As previously discussed, autism has been classified as a mental health disorder, and is almost always defined solely in terms of behavioral and developmental deficits. Usually, the more widely used definitions of autism concede that the cause of autism is not known, yet quickly assert that the condition is lifelong and incurable. For years, professionals from the medical, educational, and psychological communities ignored the physiological problems of our children as being in any way shape or form relevant to the behaviors that our children manifest. Even in recent times, in the wake of new discoveries by progressive researchers and doctors, the general view of autistic spectrum disorders (in the public and within our own community) is as incorrect as ever.

The standard definitions are *confining* rather than *defining* explanations for our children's challenges and behaviors. Still worse, they offer nothing short of dead-end, limiting beliefs and life sentences. *They offer no clue as to origin and no hope for a cure.* We can, as individuals, choose whether we want to further promote these notions of autism or, instead, set our plans of action for positive and meaningful change.

The overwhelming biological and physiological problems of our children are not even given honorable mention in many traditional profiles of autism. These can include such things as:

- ◆ Gluten/casein intolerance
- ◆ High viral antibody levels
- ◆ Gross deficiencies in vitamins and minerals (in particular Vitamin A and zinc, magnesium, B vitamins, antioxidants)
- ◆ Abnormal EEGs and seizure activity
- ◆ Abnormal thyroid levels
- ◆ Intractable diarrhea and other gastrointestinal problems, causing malabsorption of nutrients and toxin build-up
- ◆ Frequent ear infections
- ◆ Food intolerances
- ◆ Myelin Basic Protein antibodies
- ◆ Compromised immune response
- ◆ Excessive levels of toxic agents such as cadmium, lead, aluminum, mercury and other environmental toxins

♦ Abnormal urinary peptides

♦ Essential fatty acid imbalances

♦ Excessive thirst and fluid consumption

Instead, traditional definitions focus purely on abnormal social development and behavior. There is no argument that the behaviors are there. The question to ask is, *why are they there?* Most literature on autistic spectrum illness doesn't even suggest that these illnesses are the result of biological causes. *We are not led to investigate such causes.* The entire premise upon which the medical community is *acting* and, in turn, to which we as parents are *reacting*, is not valid or complete.

In addition, many professionals in the medical and psychological communities ignore the core medical needs and issues relative to our children. Consequently, they also ignore the very clues that can lead to viable research and treatment for autism. Defining our children exclusively on the basis of observed behaviors has led to several other disturbing revelations. Frequently, medical insurance policies won't pay for treatment and testing not specified for a behavioral disorder. To make matters worse, the inconsistent, inaccurate, and subjective ways in which autistic children are diagnosed by psychologists have led to a confusing and almost meaningless array of labels for our children, more like a bowl of alphabet soup than a diagnosis. The complicated array of autism labels (hence the whole "autistic spectrum" of disorders, including PDD, PDD-NOS, ADHD, Autistic, LKS, and variants of LKS), does little to help our children or us (though it may make the psychologists feel useful in the process). These labels leave us confused, desperate, hopeless, and last but not least, a divided (and therefore, further weakened) community of parents and doctors. Most importantly, the confining nature of these labels and the very definition of autism itself have served as disincentives for innovative medical research. As long as autism is considered an incurable mental disorder, funding for serious scientific study by gastroenterologists, endocrinologists, immunologists and other specialists may be limited. Interest from biotechnology firms and pharmaceutical corporations will be greatly impacted as long as the biology of autism is ignored. The reality of this unfortunate situation has put an enormous strain on the educational community, which must provide intervention for our children. The door to progress remains shut.

We cannot afford to wait until all of the systems responsible for creating a more appropriate definition of autism fall into place. Eventually, it will be our own collective strength and advocacy that will propel this change. In the interim, we must enact individual change by adopting new individual premises. *As we increase our collaboration, our individual convictions will, in the end, add up to our finest collective advocacy.*

To that end, here are some suggestions for re-creating a meaningful new premise. You may want to further refine them to best suit your child's profile.

My child's autism (or any variant name of autism)

is an inadequately explored and potentially curable illness of biological origin (perhaps, but not necessarily, including a genetic component)

in which an abnormal mechanism, problem, or complex of problems, was triggered (of neurological, endocrine, gastrointestinal, immunological, and/or metabolic nature)

at some point in development, perhaps in response to an environmental trigger (such as a vaccine) leading to biological dysfunction, causing abnormal behaviors and abnormal development to occur.

Using this model, and based upon the results of his medical testing and our own observations, here is how we eventually defined Parker's autism:

Parker's autism is an inadequately explored and potentially curable illness of biological origin, in which abnormal gastrointestinal, endocrine and immunological mechanisms or problems were triggered and have led to biological dysfunction, causing his abnormal behaviors and abnormal development to occur.

It is then helpful to enhance your new premise with information such as this:

These abnormal behaviors and development sometimes include difficulty in forming normal social relationships, problems processing language receptively and expressively, difficult-to-understand compulsive or ritualistic tendencies, and unusual mannerisms.

Finally, it is critical to include some information that will propel you into positive, purposeful action:

The outward manifestations of autism can occur in varying degrees of severity. Intense educational and biomedical intervention can often mediate these behaviors. Adequate funding for biomedical research and intense scrutiny of the physiological endpoints of various biological interventions will help direct us to an understanding of the underlying cause or causes of autistic behavior, and can potentially provide a cure one day for children such as mine who suffer from this illness.

Your new premise about autism creates real hope instead of hopelessness, and transforms fear and desperation into a new beginning. *Any* degree of autism is important (i.e., PDD is no less important than autism) and therefore any degree of autism deserves a high degree of well-targeted and aggressive biomedical and educational intervention. Any degree of autism needs the closest of medical scrutiny by open-minded and forward thinking neurologists, geneticists, endocrinologists, gastroenterologists, immunologists and the like, if we are to ever pinpoint the causes and uncover the cure.

Changing the premise does not change the child. It does not change the harsh reality of the illness. Changing the premise *does* change one of the most vital things in the process: it changes the *mission*. It is important for us to be on the *right* mission, one which will truly make a difference in our lives and, more importantly, in the health and the lives of our children.

The "Dark Ages" of autism have created a negative prognosis, which precludes a meaningful mission and purposeful actions. The adoption of a new and meaningful premise, on the other hand, provides a framework for research and an implicit indication for a useful roadmap, an appropriate navigation guide, treatment, and maybe even a cure. Not only is the adoption of a new premise empowering for parents, it is empowering for the medical, scientific, and educational communities and the special roles they play in the lives of our beautiful children. As *we* set out on the right mission, our doctors, specialists, and educators will follow.

As stated in Part I of this book, our premise changes our mission. Our mission changes our actions. Our actions will change our outcome. Outcome is everything to children and families shackled to autism. With this change in premise, our direction, our decisions, our strength, our sense of hope, our willingness to persevere, our attitude, our confidence, our relationships with doctors, educators, and friends all begin to change…in very positive and meaningful ways.

Chapter Ten

Empowerment Plan Step #2:
Charting a Roadmap

"It concerns us to know the purpose we seek in life,
for then, like archers aiming at a definite mark,
we shall be more likely to attain what we want."

~ Aristotle

In order to chart an effective roadmap for my child's recovery, I will identify the specific educational, therapeutic, and medical interventions which may be appropriate for my child in each six-to-nine-month interval. I will also identify the ways to make those interventions happen.

So often, life with children on the autistic spectrum requires almost indescribable daily management. It is difficult to get in and out of a grocery store or a mall without our children throwing a tantrum in public. We gulp down our food at home or in a restaurant to accommodate the short window of opportunity in which our children will remain seated and safely in one place. We survive the day at hand, sometimes minute-to-minute, on little to no sleep and with often no outside assistance, frequently not even from friends or family members.

One of the most emotionally charged times of my life, was the period following *Dateline NBC's* coverage of the secretin story. In the program, Parker, and his remarkable improvements after secretin infusion, were profiled. For weeks and months following the program, hundreds of letters and emails poured in. Within the first few days, we had received over 850 calls on our three phone lines. Gary and I were overwhelmed by the response, and we felt an enormous sense of helplessness, largely because we understood all too well the needs of the parents who were writing and calling. Weeks passed, and dozens of photographs mailed to us by other parents lay everywhere in our home office. These photographs of beautiful children, so full of potential, all shared one thing in common: the need for help.

Gary and I wept together as we read letter after letter, because we shared the pain and the tears that had inspired the letters and calls that we received. We wept also because there were no easy answers, no quick fixes, and no miraculous solutions to offer.

There are so many philosophies and opinions in the field of autism that it is a daunting task for any parent to sift through them all and decide on appropriate biomedical and educational interventions to pursue. Worse, most of the philosophies and opinions are, as previously discussed, wrong or woefully inadequate. Many parents have written to us, almost apologetic about their inability to tease apart the tangled web of information before them. No parent should feel embarrassed about the need for guidance in selecting appropriate help for their autistic children. It was actually this expressed need for guidance that became the impetus for sharing our personal empowerment plan with others. Step #2, *Charting a Roadmap*, outlines a few of our own suggestions (rules of thumb) for navigating down the winding paths and effectively negotiating the bumps and potholes in your field of view. As you design your own roadmap, I strongly recommend that you first try to visualize what you can accomplish inside a six-to-nine-month window. (There is nothing particularly magical about this time frame, but by choosing a finite and reasonable window of time, the process does not seem so emotionally overwhelming or strategically unmanageable.) Chart methodically and realistically. Write your strategies down on paper so that you can refer to them often and share them with like-minded people including doctors, therapists, educators, friends and other parents of autistic children. In doing so, you will stay on course and can assess your progress and realize a sense of accomplishment.

Suggestion #1

Research and identify programs for educational intervention that have been proven to be effective for children with autism. Put a plan of implementation into action that outlines specific strategies needed to establish the program of your choice for your child.

The suggestion to identify an appropriate and effective educational program is twofold in purpose. Our abilities to forge ahead, to make progress, to advocate for medical research and treatment, to become active in the empowerment process, are facilitated by our success in securing a dependable and effective educational regimen for our children. "Educational?" you ask. What about the biological foundation for autism – how do these two things fit together?

It would be preposterous to look at any child's need to learn and to communicate as being independent from the other aspects of their lives. Do we overlook or minimize the importance of teaching children with cancer, with cystic fibrosis, with AIDS, with ADHD? Of course not. Children with autism have an even more obvious need for communication, for structure, and for intense educational intervention. The underlying illness in our children creates challenges in language processing and communication that beg for serious educational and therapeutic attention.

I have been told that some proponents of certain educational philosophies have attempted to pit educational intervention and biomedical intervention against each other. If this is true, it is terribly unfortunate! I cannot think of any other illness in which this same attitude has been tolerated. Do we insist that stroke victims choose between occupational therapy and drugs? Would we make the parent of a child suffering from gastrointestinal disease, hormone and endocrine imbalances, or allergies choose between education and medical guidance? Certainly not. As absurd as these scenarios sound, that is precisely what has been reported to me by parents of autistic children. Many are made to feel quite ill at ease with regard to biomedical interventions they and their doctors may have determined to be appropriate for their children. Again, we witness the dangerous fallout from the autism myth.

Aside from the obvious merits of appropriate education for the child, it is also my contention that from a purely practical standpoint, if parents do not have an effective and organized educational program in place, their time to advocate in additional ways for their children is severely diminished. Their inability to become separated from the full-time responsibility of single-handedly trying to manage their children's challenges, impacts their effectiveness at almost everything else. It is, in essence, the proverbial "Catch 22." Absent a quality educational program for our children, both our children *and* we are rendered handicapped.

While my personal experience is with the methodology and structure of an ABA (Applied Behavioral Analysis) program, such programs are not always available or affordable. I am truly blessed to have a school district whose officials have supported Parker's educational needs every step of the way. Other philosophies of education, while different in approach and methodology, have also been effective in teaching children on the autistic spectrum.

In an ideal world, a parent would meet with the local school district officials, discuss the benefits of a particular educational program, and together they would agree upon the need for 30-40 hours per week of intensive intervention. In an ideal world, the school district would welcome and support the parent and implement the necessary and appropriate education. Of course, we hardly live in an ideal world, and the resistance to meaningful and financially feasible educational support for children with autism is legend. Though we often fantasize that our educators will be compelled to implement programs based on logical and reasonable grounds for them, the reality is that where school services are concerned, our fantasies are dashed more times than not. We uncover, in this process, yet one more obstacle in front of us.

In your goal to design and establish an appropriate educational setting for your child, you may find that you need to temporarily resort to an alternate plan of action in order to accomplish your ultimate objective. This means accepting an alternate educational setting, *with the caveat that such acceptance does not compromise your right to change courses later*. You can then use the time that your child is in such a program to appeal the school district's decision and to advocate and organize your ultimate educational objectives.

Find at least 10 hours per week that you can devote solely to reaching your goals. If there are no services for your child, you may need to find a safe child care arrangement in your home to free up your time to write letters, call attorneys, network with Easter Seals or local autism chapters and others. Using this extra time, you can determine a way to put a quality 30-40 hour per week program in place. If you are in a district where enough families do this, you will find strength in numbers as you advocate together. Sometimes, finding even 10 hours of appropriate education and safe childcare is difficult. In such circumstances, the services of caring church members, community volunteers, college students, and relatives can be sought. A team of 5 people, each offering just 2 hours per week to care for your child/children in your home while you work to set up a permanent program and a permanent intervention team, is a worthwhile approach to consider.

Your ability to research, become educated about autism and to pursue appropriate treatment and assistance is time dependent. More importantly, your child's early educational foundation is critical to his or her future well-being and progress.

As you chart your roadmap, educational interventions are the best place to begin. Lost educational opportunity is irretrievable. So is your lost time to help your child. Establishing an educational program, up front, helps your child educationally and it helps you find the time to pursue other types of intervention as well.

While your child is engaged in schooling or is being cared for in the safety of your home, you must get to a quiet, well-organized place where you are free to make phone calls, write letters, and research. (Obviously, if you have other children to care for, you may not be able to isolate yourself completely, and you can try to coordinate nap times, quiet playtime or a favorite video during this period.) Sometimes it is easier and more feasible to engage the help of a good friend or relative to make phone calls for you. You can do letter writing when your children are asleep. If you need help writing letters, other people can lend their talents in this regard, too! Don't be shy about asking other parents for copies of letters they have written for the same purpose. You will save time and energy by revising an existing letter to suit your particular circumstances.

If your school has not been cooperative in providing services for your child, use your time to procure the services you want and your child needs. Some of the following ideas may help you in changing your school's policies:

♦ Call neighboring school districts that provide high quality behavior modification programs or other quality educational services for their special-needs students. Find out:

> Who administrates and oversees the programs?

> How many hours are provided to children the same age as yours?

> Who are the therapists, how are they trained, and how much are they paid?

> How are therapists recruited? (Many parents feel that the *choice* of individual therapists is as important as the type of methodology itself.)

> How successful are the programs?

> How does the district track the success of the programs?

♦ Take detailed notes. Organize your notes so that they can be used by you, your local advocacy group, your attorney (if necessary), and your own school district.

♦ If you have access to the Internet and have an email address, become a subscriber to one of the larger autism Internet discussion groups. Get on-line and ask other parents in your geographic area to provide information about school districts that have good programs.

♦ Call your special education department, your local chapter of Easter Seals, or your local autism chapter to determine the legal advocacy groups in your area. These are usually free services, and those who provide them can accompany you to your school district meetings to support your needs.

♦ Arrange a meeting of parents in your vicinity who have similar objectives. Plan an organized approach to an appeal for services. There is strength in numbers.

♦ Gather information about the services you are requesting *before* you attempt to negotiate for those services with your school district. National or local autism chapters can help you acquire this information. Define a clear, written description of what you want your school to provide (along with a cost/benefit analysis of results over time, assuming such analysis will be in your favor). Intensive early intervention can save tens of thousands of dollars in long term, ongoing services.

♦ Always be friendly, but always be firm and never give up. Do not be disarmed by school officials who tell you that their policies don't allow for the programs that you know are the most beneficial for your child. Request that all of your school's decisions and responses to you be in writing. The officials may accede, rather than deny your rights in writing. Often, these letters can later be used to your advantage if legal action becomes necessary.

♦ Acquire copies of court cases/decisions for similar situations. Recently, many cases regarding the education of autistic children have gone to trial and the families of the children have prevailed. Provide these types of support materials to your school district officials. They are inspiring to yourself and others, and can be compelling to your school district.

Suggestion #2

Research the current and effective biomedical interventions recommended for autistic children who have similar medical profiles to your child.

Becoming knowledgeable about biomedical interventions for autism does not need to be overwhelming. The good news is that the task is easier now than ever in the past. The Internet has provided parents with ways to connect with one another and explore successful biomedical treatments.

There are some great resources to help you. The Autism Research Institute in San Diego is one of them. There are also a number of autism guidebooks that can direct your course and equip you with the knowledge you need. Two such books, which have been strongly recommended and are soon-to-be-released are: *Facing Autism: Reasons for Hope, Guidance for Help,* by Lynn M. Hamilton and *Unraveling the Mystery of Autism*, by Karyn Seroussi.[21] Presently available is Dr. William Shaw's book entitled, *Biological Treatments for Autism and PDD.* Other parents are also an excellent source of good information, as are doctors and specialists who utilize various biomedical interventions in treating autistic children. Autism web sites are rich sources of current information. These autism web sites are too numerous to list here, but with a search under "autism" on your computer, you will be guided to many of them.

To determine which specific interventions might be helpful for your child, identify the health problems that are specific to your child and write them down. Next, categorize those problems on paper, something like the example that follows:

Select the categories that may apply	Identify the physical symptoms your child or family history has	Identify the best specialists in applicable categories with phone numbers (see next page)
Gastrointestinal	Diarrhea Loose stools Constipation Vomiting Reactions to certain foods	
Endocrine	Low basal body temperature Excessive thirst Skin problems Excessive sweating Family history of thyroid problems	
Neurological	Abnormal "staring" behavior Tremors "Zoned out"	
Nutritional	Propensity for certain foods Vitamin deficiencies Poor teeth	
Immunological	Problems occur after vaccine History of frequent ear infections Allergies Rashes Red cheeks	

Suggestion #3

Research the best specialists in your geographic area for the kinds of problems you have identified in your child.

Once again, a tremendous resource is the parent network. Other parents will make recommendations for doctors in your geographical area, or for specialists outside your area who are worth a plane ticket. Although I certainly offer no medical advice regarding treatment, I think it is a good idea to wait until a full medical profile is on hand before deciding on any one type of intervention. Once you are satisfied that you have explored all of your targeted areas of concern, you are in a better position to make rational and educated decisions about potential treatment. In short, before jumping into action in any one direction, or worse, pursuing too many "scattered" directions all at once, get all of your facts in front of you so you can formulate a better overall plan of treatment for your son or daughter. (This is not to imply that you should ever withhold medical treatment if there appears to be any reason for immediate action. This is my own personal perspective, and you and your selected physicians will need to determine the appropriate measures for your child's needs.)

Suggestion #4

Prioritize, in written format, potential intervention options and then seek out the baseline testing and data you need to obtain in order to determine the appropriateness of those interventions.

Once you have selected your specialists, you are then in a position to acquire baseline data and investigate potential interventions. *If you do not approach this important step in a systematic and organized way, you may rush to put your son or daughter on a particular protocol that may exclude your option to do anything else, or to get the baseline information you really need.* For instance, if your first trip is to a neurologist who recommends that you put your child on corticosteroids and you do so, you may relinquish your option to accurately test or pursue other protocols. The presence of those kinds of drugs in your child's system may influence or contraindicate other options. If these kinds of considerations arise, ask your doctors and other parents what limitations certain treatments may pose on future options.

In addition, children who are on certain medications might not be considered candidates for an invasive procedure such as an endoscopy (scope of the intestinal tract), the results of which could prove to be enormously important in identifying information relevant to your child's health problems. Likewise, by implementing certain dietary interventions such as a strict gluten-free diet *before* something like endoscopic testing is done (if endoscopy is an eventual goal), you may sacrifice a true and complete picture of the problem from which your son or daughter may suffer. (In this example, eliminating glutens from the diet prior to a full gastrointestinal evaluation will diminish the chance that a gastroenterologist can determine if there has been damage to the intestinal villi from the glutens themselves. There is a lot of merit to implementing a gluten-free diet, and evidence that it does, indeed, contribute tremendously to the improvement of many autistic children. This is only meant to emphasize the importance of prioritizing in the planning process.) Charting your roadmap means prioritizing the testing and baseline data you need to acquire before you implement intervention and treatment. You can't bake a cake without the ingredients, and you can't effectively intervene without adequate information. Other parents and physicians, knowledgeable about the unique physiology of certain groups of autistic children, can help guide you through this process of prioritizing.

In short, while our anxiety and confusion often tempt us to try an intervention – *any* intervention – for our children, we must keep an important thing in mind. For our children's ultimate benefit, the best help that we can offer them is to be exceedingly organized, informed and logical in our approach to intervention. Formulate a comprehensive list of tests or procedures that might be helpful in selecting appropriate biomedical intervention and treatment. Be careful to stay on course and determine that any testing is purposeful to your overall objectives. Some researchers want data for their own research that may not be relevant to your purpose. While you may choose to participate in such research endeavors, make sure you know the difference between information gathered by doctors for further scientific exploration and information gathered to direct *treatment* options. And remember something else which is critically important in this endeavor: though each and every specialist has knowledge to impart, each and every parent must add to that knowledge something even greater – their *wisdom*. You may take your child to many specialists, but remember, *you* are a specialist about your child. *Don't lose confidence about the roadmap you are active in charting.* Share it (and chart it) with the help of your child's doctors and other parents with experience, and clearly articulate your thoughts and overall purpose every step of the way.

Remember our example of being on Venus, with a roadmap that leads nowhere? Deciding on medical intervention or dietary intervention with your child without first gathering all of the data will eventually put you in a maze of bewilderment, not really knowing what your next turn will be. As tempting as it is to "try it all" along the way, wait until you have a clear idea of the WHOLE picture and then decide on a path to pursue. One of the most important reasons to acquire baseline data on your child is so you will be able to measure improvement later on as you and your child's doctors select dietary and /or medical interventions appropriate for your child.

Suggestion #5

After gathering all of the baseline data sought and/or recommended for your child, and after completing your targeted testing or diagnostic evaluations on your child, the important task of determining the right treatment becomes the next priority for you and your team of medical professionals.

As I tried to determine the appropriate treatment for Parker, I decided to think of biomedical treatment and intervention in three main categories. I had the option of either **eliminating** or **supplementing** things in Parker's daily diet and treatment protocol, and I also had the option of doing **nothing**, an option that is sometimes the most prudent one under certain circumstances.

Eliminating certain foods from the diet that are offensive foods to many autistic children is a measure that carries the least risk to the child at minimal expense to the family. It is also a step that can have a tremendous impact on the child's behavior. In some children, the elimination of certain foods such as milk has caused dramatic changes in cognition, speech, eye contact and gastrointestinal function. This was absolutely true in Parker's situation.

Supplementing with vitamins, minerals, and medications is a trickier business, and it is where parents can easily become confused.

Here are just a few questions I ask myself BEFORE I add any supplements (including vitamins) to my son's regimen. You will undoubtedly add of a few of your own.

♦ Is there a good indication that my child needs this supplement? What is that indication?

♦ Have other children greatly benefited by being given this supplement? Who are they, and what changes have been noted? Are those changes relevant to my child's problems?

♦ Does the person recommending this regimen profit by that recommendation directly? (This pertains to people selling vitamins and herbal remedies in particular). If the answer to this question is "yes," it does not necessarily mean that the protocol is not valid, but it *does* mean that as a consumer, you might want to evaluate the decision more thoroughly.

♦ Will my health insurance cover this supplement? If not, is there a prescription version (as with pancreatic enzymes, for example) for which my health insurance will pay?

♦ Will this supplement interact with or void the effectiveness of any other supplements with which I wish to treat my child? If so, which is the more important of the two? From which can my child derive the *most* benefit?

♦ What benefits do I hope to see from this supplement or treatment? Can those benefits be accurately measured? How will I assess progress? How will my doctor assess progress?

♦ How soon should I expect to see benefits if the supplement is effective for my child?

♦ What risks are associated with this treatment or supplement? Are there other treatments I want to try first that carry equivalent benefits with less risks?

Here's the point: because no one has yet discovered the cause or the cure for autism, we as parents have no single treatment or medical protocol to pursue on behalf of our children. Every day, we hear of a child improving after a trial of one thing or another, and therefore it is easy to become enticed by a random approach to intervention. We want to try everything we hear about – frequently all at the same time. We are often encouraged to put our children on protocols of megavitamins, megadoses of fatty acids, anti-fungals, herbal teas, and food supplements. In reality there is, as yet, little investigation or testing following many of these regimens to validate them. While there *are* studies which clearly indicate that adding certain supplements such as B-6 and DMG brings about considerable gains in some autistic children,[22] autistic children who may have malabsorption and metabolic problems may not be able to effectively absorb or metabolize random megadoses of vitamins, minerals, and fatty acids. In short, if our children were suffering from an undetermined wound, a whole box of bandages might not stop the bleeding any better than a single bandage might. We need to be super-educated consumers. We need to ask the right questions, and we need to constantly define and refine our objectives as we pursue treatment options. The more organized and educated we are, the less overwhelmed and intimidated we will be by the professionals who evaluate and treat our boys and girls.

In April 1996, had our son been on a combination of treatments and supplements simultaneous to his secretin infusion, we would have never been able to isolate his improvements to the secretin. Worse still, it would have been nearly impossible for us to convince anyone that the secretin had been responsible for Parker's dramatic gains. Had Parker been on homeopathic remedies, herbal supplements, megavitamins, a highly specialized diet, anti-fungals and prescription drugs all at the same time, we would never have known for sure that the secretin is what had helped him.

By no means do I endorse any one particular treatment for all children, including secretin. Nor am I implying that certain diets, vitamins, anti-fungals, or supplements are in any way inappropriate. It should be noted that I offer no medical advice whatsoever. I am purely emphasizing the importance of approaching your child's diagnostic and treatment needs in a systematic way. We will undoubtedly find, in the end, that there is more than one biological etiology for autistic behavior. In fact, that is precisely part of our dilemma in treating our children and determining the causes of our children's illness. It is easy to assume that all of our children suffer from the same problem, just because they carry the same label. If you effectively re-define the description of autism and its premise to suit your child's challenges, you will, in that process, set the stage for finding effective intervention that may be entirely different from the intervention of other children who happen to share the same unfortunate behavioral manifestations. The old adage about "not judging a book by its cover" certainly applies in the world of autism. We cannot judge what is right for our individual children merely by the behaviors that they have in common.

Review:

As you attempt to uncover the causes of your child's problems, and as you investigate appropriate treatment protocols, consider the following approach with your physician:

♦ Design a systematic approach to testing, and get as much of your baseline testing completed as possible, before you initiate treatment or dietary changes.

♦ Formulate appropriate questions regarding any treatment, including all dietary supplementation and prescription drugs. Clearly define what your objectives are before entering into treatment. Later, you will know whether those objectives have been met, and can better share that information with other parents.

♦ Make sure that there is reasonable evidence that the treatment you are pursuing works. If studies have been completed, investigate whether or not those studies have been executed properly and without bias. If formal studies have not been completed, evaluate the credibility of the treatment and its potential application for your child with common sense, intelligence and information. (The results of well-executed formal studies often take many years to complete. Dr. Rimland promoted behavior modification for autistic children almost twenty years before the first formal study was completed. How many children would have missed out on this valuable intervention method had their parents waited for published results?) Determine whether the approach to treatment seems logical and safe, and whether the professional promoting it is credible. (Don't be afraid to use your own judgment, intuition and parental wisdom in assessing professionals, and don't be intimidated!)

♦ Be judicious in your efforts to try various protocols and do not employ a random approach, loading your child up with new and different things, all at once. Employ systematic, logical trials, adding one thing at a time, when reasonable. This also pertains to nutritional regimens. Understand that the effect of different nutrients can be additive, and that some things can't work at all, unless accompanied by others. Go slowly and methodically to rule out negative responses and to note positive ones. Make sure you are receiving quality advice from a licensed health care provider every step of the way. By taking this approach, you and your team of professionals will be able to discriminate precisely what helps your child and what does not. Accept gradual improvement with some interventions and don't expect overnight success.

♦ Record your child's progress so that you can expand on positive measures and avoid repeating mistakes.

♦ Be confident, always, in your relationships with medical professionals. These kinds of decisions affect your child, whom you know better than anyone. As you use your wisdom and employ your confidence, you will become more empowered. Your empowerment will help your child in innumerable ways.

Chapter Eleven

Empowerment Plan Step #3:
Implementing Empowering Beliefs

*"Thoughts are energy, and you can make your world or
break your world by your thinking."*

~ Susan L. Taylor

***I will implement a system of empowering
beliefs about my child's illness and
about autism in general, that is forward-
thinking and useful to my child, my
purpose, and my actions.***

Thoughts, energies and beliefs shape your world and your outcome.
Negative thoughts, energies and beliefs, no matter how subtle they
may be, and regardless of the source, are enemies of empowerment
and progress. They can come from every corner of the autism
community, in which we need to be working cooperatively.

Our goal, in charting and maintaining a positive course, needs to be
to avoid negative moments – moments of fear, desperation, anger,
resentment, sorrow and pain. When avoiding them becomes difficult,
we must transcend them and never harbor them, lest they destroy our

spirit, our hope and our positive energies.

Gary and I have made a habit of actually writing down the things in our lives that present negative energy, so that we can rationally address the sources of negativity, and avoid them in the future. Sometimes the sources of negative energies and beliefs come from within us. We feel vulnerable, guilty, and compromised in our abilities to help our children and to be competent parents. (Sometimes parents feel so very worn down by the ravages of autism that they even begin to assume blame themselves, just to find some kind of answer through all the chaos.)

Other times, the sources of negativity are other individuals who, by their words or actions, capture our time and our thoughts in non-productive ways. If we are to avoid the kinds of emotions and fears and anxieties brought on by others and ourselves, we need to deflect the sources of negativism and seek positive refuge. We must always be mindful that the same kind of destructive matters that invaded our relationships before autism arrived at our doorstep, are potentially even more destructive now. Negativism, gossip, innuendo, and petty disagreement are the catalysts of infection in an already open wound. They are the enemies of positive, empowering thoughts and beliefs. The small mind of negativism is not the mind of wisdom. The mouth issuing gossip is not the mouth of progress. The heart filled with hate or spite is not the heart of hope. On the surface, these things seem to have little to do with autism or its cure. Yet they have *everything* to do with our ability to use our time consistently in a positive way and to charge forward, purposefully, on a daily basis.

Having said that, I think it is almost insulting to suggest that we merely adopt what is commonly referred to as "the power of positive thinking." In reality, it is pretty hard to simply be "positive" when one's child is so seriously affected and when our lives have been so insidiously invaded by adversity. So, make no mistake about the meaning of Step #3 in this plan. It entails something much more than waking up in the morning and with a feigned smile, shouting, "I feel terrific!" right before you reach for the coffee, after a night of no sleep, preceding a day of no rest.

Step #3 suggests a fundamental shift in the way we begin to live, according to our new premise. An empowering belief is not simply a positive thought. It is a way of restructuring our daily approach to our situation in order that we will find progress instead of stagnation and success in our efforts instead of failure. It is *systematized*. It is a basis from which, on any given day, we can derive strength and wisdom. *It does not replace our basis of spiritual faith or merely create a positive attitude. It fuels us into action.*

History is full of people who formulated their own empowering belief systems. Helen Keller must have summoned up empowering beliefs with the warmth of every sunrise on her face to have accomplished what she did in the wake of tremendous challenges. In our modern day, we can witness the enormous personal strength of people such as Christopher Reeve, the famous actor rendered paralyzed after a horseback riding accident, who has not allowed his tragedy to defeat him. Each day, he must assuredly act upon a belief system that has not rendered his future worthless. We too, must adopt a belief system that is empowering, forward thinking, and useful to our actions and our goals.

Your system of empowering beliefs need not be the same as anyone else's. To be effective, however, your empowering belief system must support the new premise from which you are working, and it should relate to the circumstances for which you ultimately strive.

In the front of my daily planner, I have kept a record of many empowering beliefs, which I review almost daily. If you are a spiritual or faithful person, you might even find it helpful to incorporate the empowering beliefs you adopt into your devotion or prayer time. I find it helpful to share my empowering beliefs with God and to ask His inspiration and guidance in conceiving them and for His strength in acting upon them. Though there is room for individual expression and experience in both the creation and the content of an empowering belief system, I am confident that a positive outcome is more likely to occur for those who adopt and act upon empowering thoughts, than for those trapped in negativity.

Here are 25 excerpts from my personal notebook. Perhaps they will help to inspire you as you adopt empowering beliefs of your own.

1. No one knows what causes autism; therefore, no one can tell me with certainty that it's incurable.

2. Some children have fully recovered from autism, therefore, mine can too.

3. New information and technology are uncovered and discovered every day. This information may point to a cure, so I should seek to find it and understand it.

4. I know my child more intimately than any doctor, educator, or specialist. I have no reason to take a "back seat" in the decisions that affect him and his welfare each and every day.

5. Education and resourcefulness will help to rise above feelings of fear and helplessness, and will ultimately defeat those feelings.

6. Kind, helpful, and intelligent people are everywhere. My goal and responsibility to my child, as I seek support and information, is to find them.

7. My other (non-autistic) child can learn positive things from this unfortunate experience if I channel the situation properly. She can learn things such as compassion, patience, understanding, and unconditional love. I must use the situation to impact her life positively.

8. The best treatment for my child and the answers to all of my questions exist somewhere "out there" today. They just haven't been uncovered yet.

9. There are caring, sensitive, bright doctors and specialists who are willing to be involved and who are as eager to learn as I am. They understand my passion and concerns about my child. My goal is to find more professionals like them and encourage them to become involved.

10. My child's symptoms are really valuable clues to the causes of his autism and to his cure. My job is to tune into the clues, note both good and bad changes, and seek information and answers.

11. My child is absorbing information constantly, even when it doesn't seem obvious to me or to others. I will read to him, sing to him, smile at him, talk to him, and love him. Someday, these efforts will prove to have been worthwhile and beneficial.

12. My observations of my child are not insignificant. I will not allow words such as "subjective" or "anecdotal" (ascribed to my observations by others) diminish the importance of the observations themselves, or the valid role they play in my child's progress.

13. For generations past, the world has revealed people who overcame challenges: Helen Keller, The Pilgrims, Rosa Parks, George Washington, and Ghandi. There is nothing to prevent me from thinking as these people thought and being as these people were in spirit and in attitude.

14. I cannot always control my circumstances, but I can control how I react to them.

15. Every day can be used to bring my son closer to recovery.

16. My child is a gift, waiting to be unwrapped. My job is to untie the knots and find the seams in the wrapping.

17. My child's future begins today.

18. There are meaningful questions to ask if meaningful answers are to be found. Each day I will try to determine what those questions are.

19. There are wonderful, caring, intelligent and determined parents in my same situation. My goal is to find parents with a similar purpose to mine and to combine my strength and wisdom with theirs toward common objectives.

20. Sharing information and resources can serve to help my child and to further the greater cause. My job is to responsibly share the information and resources that I have, and to inspire other parents, doctors, researchers, educators and others to do the same.

21. My energies and abilities are different than, but equivalent to, the energies and abilities of others involved in the autism community. My job is to make sure that I contribute whatever I can to the overall cause.

22. Every member of my immediate family is an integral player in my son's recovery. My job is to identify the special roles my husband and daughter and I can each play in helping my son progress.

23. My perspective on life will forever be changed by autism and will provide more clarity of purpose and meaning to everything I do.

24. I was made with an infinite amount of love to give, and I should constantly give it to others around me.

25. My individual empowerment in the face of autism makes a huge difference in the collective search for the cure.

Some of this material will also be contained in other areas of the book. The key word in the title of this chapter is ***implementing***. Empowerment is about putting good thoughts and positive energy into ***action***. However, without the right attitude and belief system, even the right method may not work.

Along with *implementing* the positive, we need to reduce and eliminate the stressful things that can thwart our good motives and interfere with our empowering beliefs. In the next chapter, I will discuss this in more detail.

Chapter Twelve

Empowerment Plan Step #4:
Eliminating Little Sources of Stress

"Small stresses often have big shadows."

~ Gary Beck

As much as possible, I will eliminate the little stresses in my life that can potentially add to the larger stresses. I will try to employ the "Six Stress Savers" in my interactions with others!

Autism is a BIG deal. It is unlike divorce. It is unlike the loss of a business. One cannot leave it behind and start over. Autism is constantly *in your face*, every day. At one moment, it is like being hit by a Mack truck. At another moment, it is like sand in the bottoms of a pair of shoes. Whether it hits hard at any given moment or subtly wears one down, it is a BIG deal, indeed, and places an enormous stress on everyday life, everyday things, everyday thoughts, and everyday feelings.

Today's fast-paced, hectic lifestyles bombard us with stress levels of heightened proportions. Add autism to the already overflowing pot of "typical" stress, and an overwhelming level of chaos, pain, and stress can occur. Why? Because often

> ...a child with autism cannot understand the language that communicates information, instructions, danger, learning, and life in general.

> ...a child with autism often behaves wildly out of control at home and in public places, throwing tantrums to communicate his or her needs and wants.

> ...a child with autism often cannot participate in many of the social activities of family life, even those that require only a modicum of social compliance.

> ...a child with autism is often denied the educational services he or she needs, and cannot be integrated into typical classroom settings.

> ...a child with autism typically doesn't reciprocate the love extended to him or her by others in an overt or customary fashion.

> ...there is no public place to comfortably go with most autistic children, little hope offered for an autistic child, inadequate educational and research funding for an autistic child, and few biomedical treatments readily available for an autistic child.

> ...children with autism often have difficulty establishing normal sleeping or eating patterns.

> ...children with autism frequently do not become toilet-trained until they are older.

...children with autism, in addition to their behavioral and developmental challenges, often have medical challenges and issues such as compromised immune function.

It is almost impossible to ignore the plain reality of autism, and the resulting damage it heaps upon our personal lives, our professional lives, our relationships, and our families. One of the keys to surviving the *big* challenge of autism is in the effective management of the *small* things that seem to magnify the larger problem. The quality of our lives correlates, in part, to our ability to eliminate, deflect, and re-direct the little stresses that can make the major issues seem even worse.

There is a host of big stress that we encounter daily. Little stresses can slowly erode the landscape of progress we try so hard to build. At every turn, the smallest of issues can ignite tremendous anxiety. What *are* some of these small issues? Here are just a few familiar ones:

◆ A careless comment tossed out by a stranger in a grocery store who doesn't know the illness that causes your child's behavior.

◆ The ignorance of a relative who believes your child is out of control because of your poor parenting.

◆ The inability to always maintain household neatness and order, or to consistently cook a family meal because autism has stolen your time and energy from such tasks.

◆ Comments from others regarding how "hard" their days are, how "difficult" their typical kids can be, how "tired" they feel on any given day.

◆ Comments from other parents or professionals within the autism community itself, who differ philosophically regarding educational approaches and biomedical treatment choices or are just unkind about the job you are trying to do with your child.

The list is endless, and one of the questions we must ask ourselves is, "What can I do to effectively minimize these smaller issues (or, better yet, dispose of them altogether) in order to improve quality of life for myself and my family and maximize my strengths and energy?"

Naturally, there are differences among us regarding the sources of our stress. For me, managing my expectations of the people in my personal relationships was the most difficult hurdle to leap. I spent a lot of time during the first year of Parker's illness feeling disappointed and angry with family members and friends. I wanted to believe that, had their child been the one in need, I would have offered to help research or make phone calls, or fold laundry or make dinner every once in awhile, just to ease the pain and anguish. But the situation was what it was. All of my fantasizing didn't change it, and my expectations only served a negative purpose. Until I learned to change my own expectations of others, such expectations were a source of stress that frequently got in the way of positive action. I will discuss the subject of our expectations of others in the pages ahead, and will touch on five other types of little stresses as well, that can affect our lives negatively.

Gary grouped these types of stresses into six categories that he called our "Six Stress Savers." When we conceived the plan, he felt that by identifying and categorizing the little daily stresses (the sand in the shoes), we could more effectively take positive action against them. We could determine ways to deflect a lot of the stress before it took root in our home or our relationship with one another. His six categories are listed here, and then individually discussed in more detail.

Gary's "Six Stress Savers"

1. *Expectations of Others*

I will recognize that the expectations I have of other people can be a huge source of my own little stresses. I should try to manage those expectations, because in doing so, I will eliminate much of my stress.

2. *Expectations of Self*

The expectations I have of myself need to be appropriate, given my circumstances.

3. *Organization/Time Management*

My organization and time management skills are central to keeping a focused mind and to minimizing the stress that disorganization and wasted time can ultimately cause.

4. *Targeting Actions*

I should target my actions in ways that will foster goodness within me and promote progress for my child.

5. *Managing Feelings and Emotions*

I will not deny my feelings and emotions, but I will strive to manage them and share them with the right people, to the right degree, for the right purpose, in the right way.

6. *Nurturing Important Relationships*

I will nurture only personal and professional relationships that serve a positive purpose in my life and the life of my family.

Stress Saver #1 – Expectations of Others

"I will recognize that the expectations I have of other people can often be a huge source of my own little stresses. I should try to manage those expectations, because in doing so, I will eliminate much of my stress."

The expectations we have of others can be boomerangs of stress in disguise. When our child is sick and his or her resulting behavior is out of control, when our lives are turned upside-down by this illness called autism, many of us have expectations that our relatives, friends, church members, neighbors, and co-workers will be able to intuitively recognize our need for support and help, and will readily supply both. Even if they don't recognize it intuitively, our explicit descriptions of nights without sleep, days on end without a break, medical testing without insurance, and school systems with inadequate services should send a resounding cry for help that *anyone*, especially those close to us, would understand, right? Not so.

The right kind of assistance and support from others should always be gratefully accepted and appreciated. But it is the unrequited expectation of assistance and support that leaves us resentful, angry and disappointed. Our negative feelings can become harbored deep within us and tend to fester and re-surface repeatedly at inappropriate moments. These little annoyances manifest themselves as STRESS.

Even when we are able to articulate the exact help and support we need, we cannot control the response that others will have to our plight. When a physician or educational therapist fails to meet our expectations, we have the option of replacing that professional. This is not readily an option with friends, relatives or co-workers. If the people who make up our personal life do not meet our expectations, we may need to modify our expectations of them and find alternate ways to get our goals met.

Several years back, I decided that the disappointment *I had* regarding other people, didn't really affect those other people at all. It hurt me. Not only did their failure to help and support me leave my situation the same, my anger and resentment about their failure to help made my situation worse! I became stressed about something that was probably never going to change. Instead of setting up expectations that were unrealistic, I made a conscious effort to simply be grateful for any positive support and encouragement that came my way. I have truly eliminated an enormous amount of stress in so doing.

When we allow feelings of anger and resentment to invade our hearts, we become less able to use our thoughts and our feelings in a positive way, toward the progress and future of our children. The "poor me" attitude is a vicious, self-fulfilling cycle of negative energy. Negative energy does not enable. It cripples.

Stress Saver #2 – Expectations of Self

> *"The expectations I have of myself need to be appropriate, given my particular circumstances."*

This statement does not, in any way, imply that we are merely victims of circumstance, powerless in our mission and impotent in our actions! Assessing the expectations we have of ourselves starts with understanding our goals clearly as we begin each and every day. We need to make sure that our goals are realistic, and we need to evaluate our progress at the end of the day, according to the initial goals we have set for ourselves.

For instance, if our goal at the beginning of the day is to write letters and make phone calls advocating the implementation of an educational program, which is going to take 6 hours, then setting an expectation that the house be in perfect order and a gourmet meal be prepared for dinner may be very unrealistic.

When autism invades our lives, we need to accept that the new challenges alter both the time and the emphasis that we once placed on other things. If we try to keep things status quo, and simply add all the additional responsibilities that come with our child's illness on top of the pile, we set up a plan for added stress in the process.

Don't become irritated with yourself if the house is a little more disordered than usual, or if dinner is less elaborate than it once used to be. Instead, if you have accomplished other worthwhile goals for day, delight in your progress.

The expectations that we have for ourselves do not need to cause stress for us if the expectations are appropriate to our circumstance. When our children's future welfare re-defines our goals and objectives for each new day, it becomes necessary to temporarily shed the expectations and priorities we once had under different circumstances. Think of it this way: you have a greater cause than you once had. Your agenda has a different meaning than one you may have had in the past. Don't allow unrealistic expectations of yourself to add to the big deal of life with autism. Place positive value on the accomplishments you make every day, as you work toward the recovery of your child.

Stress Saver #3 – Organization/Time Management

> *"My organization and time management skills are central to keeping a focused mind and to minimizing the stress that disorganization and wasted time can ultimately cause."*

Among the things important to families affected by autism, organization and time management skills are central. When autism comes bounding through our doors, it wreaks havoc in many ways. In the midst of our children's erratic behaviors and general chaos in our day-to-day schedules, we must find some way for our efforts and our advocacy to become ordered and organized. To fail at this important step is to seriously compromise our abilities to stop our lives from spinning out of control. We must transcend the "unordered" nature of the illness itself if we are to conquer it.

Here are some of the measures we employed that maximized our progress, our time, and our working conditions. Undoubtedly, every person's personal circumstances render their own plan of organization unique. Perhaps you will be helped by a few ideas you may not have tried in the past.

♦ Set aside quiet time (15 minutes) each day to plan your goals and to add detail to your overall objectives.

♦ Write down the goals and objectives that define your plan. Prioritize your goals and objectives and your other activities for the day.

♦ Establish the resources you need to carry out your plan and utilize those resources effectively. For instance, if you need to research a particular topic, investigate whether your local research librarian or your local "nurse" or "medical" hotline can help you find the answer you need more quickly. This will save you valuable time.

♦ Eliminate sources of interference in your day. This means getting rid of extraneous phone calls, idle chat on the Internet, and conversations with others that serve no real positive purpose. *Avoid the impulse toward escapism.* Utilizing your time to your child's advantage will eliminate the chances for your stress level to escalate because of wasted hours.

♦ Clearly communicate your plan to others, if it helps them to respect your time, and especially if other people can facilitate your goals.

♦ Do things that are important rather than things that choose you! For me, this means scheduling in advance the time I intend to spend on the telephone and on-line reading email. Both tend to side-track my focus and steal my time.

♦ Learn to schedule mindless tasks such as folding laundry and emptying the dishwasher or ironing clothes when your phone time is scheduled. I allow up to only two hours daily of telephone time, and I make sure to save up mindless tasks for the same scheduled time. Do two things at once and "double" your progress without doubling your time! In general, shaping your time will shape your outcome.

♦ Schedule time each day to organize and file your notes and letters. This time, while often hard to find, will make the critical difference in your ability to maximize your efforts.

♦ Condense your weekly chores. Become more efficient at things such as grocery shopping and the necessary tasks of everyday living. I have found that by planning 25 healthy dinner menus on 3x5 cards (dinners that can each be prepared in 30 minutes), I make lots more time for autism advocacy and research. I keep those cards with me on grocery trips so that I am less stressed out in the store, when I am struggling to manage the children and the grocery shopping simultaneously.

♦ Know what kind of help to ask for, and be willing to accept it only if it serves *your* objectives and goals. If a family member generously offers to do your wash or make a meal to free up your time, make sure they understand that you can not be available for idle chat or other problems. Keep your friends and family focused!

♦ Don't take on other "monkeys." This is one of Gary's frequent admonitions to me. Even though your good nature may make you want to be sensitive to the trials and tribulations of others, make sure that you don't become *absorbed* by other people's burdens, especially burdens for which you have no solutions. This does not mean to be insensitive or unkind to others. Simply know where to draw the line when others want to use up your time in counterproductive ways. Don't feel guilty! You must keep sight of your important mission and your plan – for your child's sake and for your own sanity.

Keep your plans simple and lean. Stay on course, and stay organized. These few things will help you to work at peak levels and to maintain your personal focus as you become empowered to help your child.

Stress Saver #4 – Targeting Actions

"I should target my actions in ways that will foster goodness within me and promote progress for my child."

Booker T. Washington once said, "If you want to lift yourself up, lift up someone else." This *does not* mean take on their problems! It does mean that we should never underestimate the positive energy that can come from doing a kind deed, sending some warm words, or sharing a wonderful moment with others. Look for inspiration every day, and target your behaviors. It will reduce the stress you feel. You will become how you act!

If you act hopeful, you will be more hopeful.
If you act thankful, you will be more grateful.
If you act enthusiastic, you will feel more energetic.
If you smile a lot, you will feel happier.
If you hug and kiss your children and spouse a lot, you will feel more loving.
If you act confident, you will reduce your anxiety and fear.
If you express yourself intelligently, you will feel smart.
If you get organized, you will be able to work in an organized manner.

Our actions must parallel our goals. Our actions serve to re-fuel us as much as they serve to fuel our purpose.

For instance, I have made it a practice to tell the special educators and the school officials at Parker's school how grateful I am for all of the support they have rendered in certain areas of Parker's program. It doesn't mean that we haven't disagreed on other issues. We certainly have, on numerous occasions. However, emphasizing my gratitude makes me feel positive coming away from the meeting, and probably makes the school feel positive and rewarded regarding Parker's educational program. The stress is reduced in all directions.

I've also made a point of taking ten minutes here and there to write small notes of thanks to the doctors who have been helpful to us along the way. We often forget how important it is for these truly dedicated professionals to feel appreciated, and it reminds me, through the action of writing the note, that I have some terrific people on my team – on Parker's team. Knowing that brings tremendous comfort. My comfort reduces my stress.

We have also found that the simple act of saying grace before each and every meal in our house can turn off a moment of stress, and make us reflect upon our blessings, not solely upon autism.

Actions are, in a way, a "stress compass." They point you in an uplifting or a stressful direction. Which direction you travel will either empower you toward progress or drag you toward desperation. Whether the action is a small one or a monumental one, all actions work together to form a picture of how life unfolds each day. Try to make that picture a work of art!

Stress Saver #5 – Managing Feelings and Emotions

"I will not deny my feelings and emotions, but I will strive to manage them and share them with the right people, to the right degree, for the right purpose, in the right way."

There is a quotation by Aristotle that I keep tucked away in my planner. Here it is:

"Anybody can become angry – that is easy; but to be angry with the right person, and to the right degree, and for the right purpose, and in the right way- that is not within everybody's power and is not easy."

Obviously, this quotation deals specifically with the emotion of anger, but it can be generalized to remind us to manage our emotions toward others, and within ourselves. Notice that Stress Saver #5 does not say *deny* your feelings, but instead, *manage* them.

The important message is for us to manage our feelings, instead of allowing our feelings to manage us. All of us cry. All of us, whether burdened with autism or not, have had wretched days, filled with pain and sorrow and anguish. We have days when we feel weak and unable to cope. The range of feelings that we experience is part of the human condition. Considering how challenging autism is for our children and for our lives, it is to be expected that we would all experience a very full range of emotions on an ongoing basis. To express those feelings is natural. To allow those feelings to irrationally direct our daily agenda, however, is useless.

Several years ago, Gary had been on a business trip, a fairly typical occurrence in his job. I had been on my own with both children for several days. Parker had been at his worst, not sleeping except a few hours during the night, non-verbal, behaviorally out of control and physically very sick, not yet potty trained, and with constant diarrhea.

We had recently moved to New Hampshire. It had been our fifth major relocation in three years. I was sleep-deprived, and exhausted. I had not lived in the new house long enough to make friends in the neighborhood and had no help from family members. It was a period of time when almost daily I would find myself in tears in the grocery store, or the dry cleaners, or driving behind the wheel of my car. As I tried to sign up my daughter in neighborhood activities I broke down and cried as I looked at all the other "normal" boys and girls. But this particular week, while Gary was traveling, everything seemed to culminate in an absolute flood of inconsolable sobbing. Gary felt helpless in his absence from home. I felt almost paralyzed in my lack of ability to put one foot in front of the other.

From his hotel room, unbeknownst to me, Gary called Kathy, the mom of a child like Parker, thinking that perhaps she could help to comfort me, long distance, on the phone. Gary reasoned that she knew what I was feeling – she had been there once herself. Her child had nearly recovered, and Gary knew I had a lot of respect and admiration for her. She called me and we spent a long time talking. Her wonderful sense of humor also made me laugh. It did help. It helped to know I wasn't the only one who had ever felt so low, and it helped to laugh. After that grand emotional meltdown, as I call it, I realized that what had happened to me was one of the most destructive aspects about autism. I had allowed *it* to control *me*. Autism was going to win, if I could not manage my feelings.

Just as Aristotle says about anger, we need to learn to manage *all* of our feelings and emotions to the right degree, for the right purpose, and in the right way. It is not easy, but if our goal is to beat autism, autism cannot beat us first.

So, how do we manage the feelings we all will inevitably have? How do we keep our feelings from spiraling out of control and weakening our resolve?

The most effective way to manage feelings is to change our mental state through our *actions*. We become active in the process, instead of passive.

One of the ways my friend Kathy was able to help me, was by listening and letting me know she understood my pain. However, she also got me laughing on the phone with her. That simple step didn't change my problem, but it shifted my emotion and it changed my mental state.

Here are some other ideas to help in managing your emotions by your actions.

♦ Avoid sad songs about broken hearts or romance-gone-bad. Listen to upbeat, "happy" music. Gary and I have created and sponsored a Benefit Music CD project called *Stand Up! Speak Out!,* inspired by our belief that our positive actions in the face of adversity are our most important allies. Music can lift up our hearts and evoke a real sense of purpose within us.

♦ Change your emotional state by changing your physical state. Physical exercise of *any* kind can boost your state of mind. Making the time for formal exercise programs can be nearly impossible with the full-time responsibilities of an ill child. If it is at all possible, a walk outside, a bike ride, five minutes on a treadmill a few times per day, or any kind of physical play activity with your child can be therapeutic for your emotional state.

♦ Do something to keep yourself involved in the achievement of your goals. Research something you've identified as being important in your child's illness. Write a letter to a public official about one of the many important issues that affect our children. Sometimes, just being engaged in the process can change your mental state.

Obviously, feelings are personal, and so are the ways you can choose to manage them. In general, however, if you begin to recognize your negative, dis-empowering feelings as signs for action on your part, those feelings will not render you helpless, fearful, and stressed. Don't allow the stress of grief, hurt, anger, fear, and worry to be the enemies to your strength in your fight for a cure.

Stress Saver #6 – Nurturing Important Relationships

"I will nurture only personal and professional relationships that serve a positive purpose in my life and the lives of my family and children."

This last stress saver is, in some ways, a culmination of many of the steps that precede it. The operative word here is *important*. It doesn't say nurture *all* relationships, only *important* ones.

Important personal relationships and professional relationships with others can ultimately help your child. In addition, they can provide a wonderful source of comfort to you and your family. Non-important and negative personal and professional relationships can be a source of stress, and a waste of your precious time and energies.

Relationships that serve a positive purpose in your life and the life of your child need to be cherished and nourished. Over the past 5 years, autism has prompted Gary and me to re-evaluate all of the relationships in our lives. To our surprise, our interactions with certain people needed to undergo a drastic shift in the new context of our lives. Autism changes lives and perspectives, for both the family it affects and the people involved with that family. We gave up trying to hold on to friends who had no understanding or tolerance for our *new* life – life with a special-needs child. We stopped trying to make excuses for family functions or get-togethers or group vacations that were no longer conducive to our lifestyle. Instead, we identified relationships that weren't stressful to maintain and relationships conducive to our new purpose. We nurtured *them*, instead.

Being able to distinguish important from unimportant relationships and then taking the actions needed to foster the important, positive ones, relieved us of needless stress. It also made more time for meaningful friendship and the facilitation of our efforts by people who truly cared. The result was less stress and more progress.

Chapter Thirteen

Empowerment Plan Step #5: Using Knowledge and Wisdom

"Knowledge without wisdom is weak and useless, and knowledge without integrity is dangerous and dreadful."

~ adapted from Samuel Johnson

After love and prayer, knowledge and wisdom used together are the two most powerful tools I have to help my child recover.

In the past, the medical advocacy of parents was limited by a lack of readily available scientific and medical information. Today, the Internet has facilitated parents of autistic children by opening up these gates of information and knowledge. It has also enabled parents to find each other, to share the information we discover and to combine our individual wisdom about our children and autism.

The wisdom and intelligence of our collective body, combined with the new availability of scientific knowledge and medical information, culminates in a powerful and even intimidating force, never before felt as it is today.

Many parents are finally beginning to realize the active role they can play in the medical treatment of their autistic children. Autism affects so many systems and functions in our children's body. No *one* single physician, especially in the context of all of the other medical knowledge he or she is expected to possess, can devote the necessary amount of time to researching all of the medical problems our children have. Some of our children's symptoms never reveal themselves in the span of a half-hour evaluation. In addition, autism can affect multiple body systems, not covered by any *one* medical discipline. We cannot expect our doctors to be specialists in our particular child. *But we should expect that they respect the information and contributions about our own children that we provide to them. We have valuable knowledge and wisdom to offer. We are motivated to research topics about which our doctors may not have strong interest.*

We may not have advanced degrees, and we may not even have undergraduate degrees. But as parents, we *do* have initials after our names that we may never have realized were there: not M.D., not Ph.D., but "I.M. (as in *I am*)" Those initials mean everything to your child. They mean "I.M." my child's mom (or dad). They mean "I.M." able to see things every day that are clues to my child's illness that no one else has the opportunity to capture. They mean "I.M." motivated, dedicated and activated in a way that only someone living with autism each and every day can possibly understand. They mean "I.M." as worthy of respect and consideration as any other specialist or professional (provided I am educated, reasonable and rational about the subject at issue).

It is imperative that we do our part in acquiring the knowledge and displaying the wisdom that is needed in order to play an integral role in uncovering the cause and finding a cure for our children. Even though the systems all around us may falter, *we must not fail ourselves*. The information available to us today, equips us with some of the most powerful tools in our arsenal. Never underestimate the value of the knowledge you can acquire via the Internet, other educated parents, like-minded, biomedically-oriented physicians, autism workshops and seminars, medical journals, and the good, old-fashioned library shelf. The more educated we become, the stronger we are. Become knowledgeable about your options and use your wisdom to look critically at those options as they apply to your child and you.

Here are some suggestions to increase your knowledge of important topics in autism if you are starting out, starting over, or starting to become empowered in your journey. Some of these have been mentioned before, in other sections.

- ♦ Write or fax the Autism Research Institute (4182 Adams Avenue, San Diego, CA 92116, fax (619) 563-6840) and request their latest information packet on autism. The best source of information they offer on the newest developments is their newsletter, which is both inexpensive and invaluable.

- ♦ Purchase one of the incredible new autism "guidebooks" that have recently come on the market (the Autism Research Institute's newsletter often reviews and recommends good books).

- ♦ Use the Internet to become informed and connected to other parents and doctors.

- ♦ Use a good search engine on the Internet to investigate studies on issues that affect your child. Don't overlook the importance of trying to make connections to other illnesses or disorders that run in your family. Keep notes of these in your files and report familial connections to your doctor regarding thyroid disorders, autoimmune disorders, gastrointestinal and endocrine disorders, vitamin A deficiencies (such as night blindness) celiac disease, cystic fibrosis, schizophrenia, ADHD, and epilepsy. These things may have significance and may prompt more in-depth investigation, if patterns or connections are made frequently enough. Share these connections with other parents.

♦ Invest in at least one good, easy-to-read, medical physiology book. My personal favorite is *Guyton & Hall's Textbook of Medical Physiology* by Arthur C. Guyton, M.D. and John E. Hall, Ph.D. It discusses complicated topics in understandable terms, and has wonderful illustrations. Research scientist Dr. David Gregg recommended it to me. I am grateful to him every time I refer to it.

♦ Purchase some comprehensive medical software for your home computer. Many good programs are available.

♦ Attend conferences that provide information on the biomedical underpinnings of autistic spectrum disorders.

Once we have armed ourselves with knowledge, the question in front of each and every one of us, whether we are parents, researchers, educators or doctors, needs to be:

*"How can I **contribute**?" instead of "What, or whom, can I **control**?"*

The autism community has been polarized, fragmented, and tremendously weakened by those who seek to control for selfish ends. The desire to control pits parents against each other, doctors against their colleagues, parents against doctors, and autism organizations against one another. Ultimately, it positions us all against real progress for our children. It keeps us, metaphorically speaking, on the "dark side of Venus."

By continuously seeking to contribute the knowledge we have, in a responsible way, we will, together, find the answers we need to eradicate the illness from which our children suffer. If instead, knowledge is used as a means of control, we have turned the clock back to autism's past.

Enthusiasm can be an empowering attribute, and enthusiasm for a particular agenda can be a good thing. That enthusiasm should never cross the line toward control by attempting to stifle other legitimate paths. In like manner, our knowledge should never be used *against* others, as a means of control. Such control is devastating to our children in the long run.

My plea goes out to parents, educators, physicians and psychologists alike: contribute your knowledge in every positive way you can. Reject the urge to control others, and reject others who are trying to control. Knowledge, wisdom and contribution, not control, are what will help us find the answers we seek.

Chapter Fourteen

Empowerment Plan Step #6:
Networking with Facilitation Partners

"No matter what accomplishments you make,
somebody helps you."

~ Althea Gibson Darben

> ***I will build upon my foundation of***
> ***facilitation partners, network with them***
> ***regularly and will keep records of positive***
> ***interventions and strategies that may***
> ***relate to my child or my family.***

When I commenced writing this chapter, I turned to my personal diary, and quickly realized that I would be hard pressed to summarize even a smattering of the knowledge or the depth and breadth of information that has been passed on to me by others. The pages are rich with scribbled notes from my conversations with friends and talented professionals who have generously given their time, their knowledge and their hearts to the cause so near to my own heart – autism. As the clock on my office wall has ticked late into the night, these people, whose names will always be hallowed in my soul, have offered their unreserved personal and intellectual honesty, advice and friendship, experience and knowledge. They have sharpened my own thought processes and empowered my resolve. They have enriched the process of learning immeasurably. Their help and insights have made the critical difference in making the secretin connection. They are what I term my *facilitation partners*, and the exchange of friendship, knowledge, respect and wisdom that we have had with one another has been very important to the process of my own empowerment. They have shared their own networks of facilitation partners with me, not out of any self-serving purpose but rather out of our common desire to find real answers for the future of children on the autistic spectrum. My diary of facilitation partners is the most important and valuable research book on my shelf.

I visualize facilitation partners like pieces of railroad track on the roadmap. Every conversation, every encounter, every moment spent with our facilitation partners brings us closer to our destination. Some of the pieces come from different angles and perspectives. Some of the knowledge and information fits neatly together. Some of it doesn't seem, at first glance, to fit at all. Eventually, huge pieces of the track are formed, which ultimately lead in a common direction. Surrounding oneself with the right facilitation partners is essential, because where all of us need to get, collectively, is beyond the capacity of any one of us, individually.

Ernest H. Starling (the co-discoverer of the secretin hormone) said these important words in 1923:

> *"...it must be remembered that the ordered knowledge of the world around us, whether living or dead, which we call science, forms a connected whole; and though, as its line advances, a brilliant discovery may push one part of the line in advance of the rest, such an outpost must remain more or less in the air and incapable of further advance until the whole line has moved up to its support."*[23]

We must facilitate one another in our learning and our efforts, respecting rational, progressive thought, even when it may seem far out or extreme. The idea of using secretin to treat autism was so radical to the dozens of specialists and researchers we initially contacted that we were largely ignored. When there exists good reasoning behind a novel idea, however, a team of facilitation partners can make all the difference in whether that idea or theory dies or survives. Facilitators build tracks over, around, and often even *through* the negative obstacles, with the goal of forming a "connected whole," as Starling so aptly puts it.

Unfortunately, there are still too many people who are willing to watch others build the track, reserving their time and contributions for criticism, cynicism and skepticism. I call this second group the *debilitation partners*, for although on some level they share in the same problem, they do not share in the solution. This is the group that puts obstacles *on* the tracks of progress. This is the group that always can share what they think in hindsight, but can offer little insight along the way. There is so much yet to be learned, and in learning, we must do all that we can to facilitate and help as we strive for the advancement of the line in which we all stand.

How does one develop a core group of facilitation partners on their journey to empowerment? More importantly, how does one become a facilitation partner to others? Here are a few ideas that have been helpful for me in the past. Some of them may be applicable to you. Whether your efforts lead you to general autism research or are primarily focused on your own child's needs, your circle of facilitation partners is important and some of these ideas will apply.

1. Make a list of the information you need and why you need it. Eliminating superfluous information will help you maximize your time and will streamline the discussion you have with others. Know what your purpose is, and

don't stray from that purpose when you ask others for their time and knowledge.

2. *Do your homework.* Facilitation partners are not meant to be the abridged editions to information about autism readily available through other means. Respect the time of your partners.

3. Make a list of the people you think can facilitate the specific question or targeted goal you have identified.

4. Always make sure that there are no distractions when you are requiring someone else's time and help. This is often difficult while caring for an autistic child. Try to schedule a time with the person when you know you will be able to devote your full attention. I make my calls at night when the children are asleep. I schedule them during the day by calling or emailing and asking if evenings are an acceptable option for the other person. Keep the conversation on target. Don't gossip. Take notes. Jot down suggested references and follow up on them.

5. Ask open-ended questions and then listen to what your facilitation partners have to say. You have not called them to promote your beliefs.

6. If your goal is to learn and to find answers for your child, then all discussions should be handled in an atmosphere of openness and trust. Anyone who is not trustworthy should not be in your circle of facilitators. Share your theories along the way with others in the same spirit of openness. Take the time to write your thoughts and ideas on paper. The most valuable piece of advice Dr. Rimland ever gave me was several weeks after Parker's endoscopy. He told me to put my thoughts, theories, and ideas down in writing. In doing so, I refined my thinking, and had a tool that proved to be very useful in tapping into dozens of professionals who may not have otherwise ever bothered to give the secretin connection serious consideration.

7. Provide recognition to those who deserve it. It is always right to give credit where credit is due. In doing so, you will inspire others to continue to work in a positive manner to find more information.

8. Determine how you can make the relationship mutually supportive. A willingness to help out with a partner's research endeavors will further your own knowledge and bolster theirs. Teamwork is desperately needed within the autism community, if further advancement is to be realized. Try to network and connect other people who have complementary research interests. Make a habit of always asking your facilitators for recommendations of helpful books, literature, resources, and doctor's names. Likewise, pass along such recommendations to others to help them in their search for good information.

9. Develop a detailed, written profile on your child. This should include a clinical history in summarized form, and your impressions regarding those things that describe or affect your child. (Your assessment of your own child is important and *valuable*! Do *not* reserve comments that you think are important, merely because you think a certain medical professional seeing them won't agree with you.) A written profile propels you in a powerful way toward finding the answers to the problems you've identified. Having the profile on hand will save time and streamline your endeavors with multiple physicians and specialists, all of whom want the same background information on your child's medical history. You can email or fax this information ahead of time to facilitate phone calls and reduce lengthy verbal explanations in your conversations with others.

10. Draw a "map" of where you envision your facilitation network to lead. This exercise will help direct your efforts and broaden your scope of thinking. We drew a map leading to Parker's endoscopy among other things. Putting the goal in a physical format helped to identify whom we needed to contact and what we needed to do in order to reach our goal.

11. Touch base regularly with facilitators to maintain relationships and to continually share what you've learned along the way. You always have something important to offer. Give thought to what that is before you call someone

12. Be respectful and trustworthy with sensitive information given to you by others. Confidentiality regarding sensitive information should always be assumed and upheld to the best of your ability. Privacy issues are important in any relationship, but especially important among families facing autism.

13. Empowerment and progress have little to do with personal confrontation and negative energy. As a general rule, don't use your energies to try and persuade others who have unmovable opposing points of view. Instead, utilize your positive energies to investigate, and assist the cause about which you are passionate. Leave the negative energies in the dust.

14. Get on the Internet! Internet discussion groups that are designed to share information and resources about biomedical interventions, treatments, and research are a rich source of facilitation partners. I have met some of the most knowledgeable and helpful parents and professionals this way.

Chapter Fifteen

Empowerment Plan Step #7:
Asking Meaningful Questions

*"Millions saw the apple fall,
but Newton was the one who asked why."*

~ Bernard Baruch

Only meaningful questions will be permitted in my daily journey with my child. I will encourage the same from those around me, including family members and specialists, because these questions will ultimately determine the answers I will find.

It is the *hows* and the *whys* and the *what ifs* that have been responsible for some of the most inspiring discoveries and significant breakthroughs of the scientific world. No doubt it will be these same little words that ultimately lead to the cure for autism.

Imagine the kinds of empowering questions that must have preceded the description of the vein-artery system by William Harvey in the seventeenth century or the construction of the mercury thermometer by Gabriel Fahrenheit in the early eighteenth century. Can you also imagine the kinds of empowering questions that must have motivated the founders of the International Red Cross in 1864, or the kinds of questions that culminated in the production of aspirin in 1899? What were the questions that tapped the brilliance of Ernest Rutherford, who split the atom in 1919, or the questions that Flemming asked in 1928 that transformed medical treatment with his discovery of penicillin in a mold? We can only imagine, because, of course, we don't know for certain. But as we wonder, we can also recognize the power of questions themselves. At the core of every great discovery are empowering questions, which may be as simple as, "Why did that happen?" and an empowering attitude which creates positive actions and results.

The nature of our questions can either lead us to new connections or make us the victims of old directions. There is much potential for greatness when even fairly ordinary people ask extraordinary questions and are motivated to find answers where none existed before.

As I discussed in the last chapter, our facilitation partners are like pieces of railroad track, each working together to form a connected whole. The questions we ask along the way, if they are meaningful, rational, educated, and serve a positive purpose, combine to form the engine on that track. It is an engine powerful enough to climb the steepest mountain, engineered well enough to round the sharpest curves, and tough enough to withstand the worst of storms. In like manner, if questions are meaningless, irrational, uneducated, and negative, a faulty engine is produced, an engine that is likely to veer off into disaster and doom or to sit, rusting in the rail yard.

Parents of autistic children have been led off the cliffs of doom and disaster on many an occasion. We have been betrayed both by the *refusal* of others to ask the *right* questions about autism for the right reasons, and by their insistence on asking the wrong questions for the wrong reasons.

The potential role of vaccines in our children's illness is a case in point. Many government officials, physicians, pharmaceutical manufacturers and others are refusing to ask this important question. "Is it plausible, given the timing of the onset of autistic symptoms and evidence of physical involvement such as compromised immune function, seizures, high viral antibodies and gastrointestinal problems, that vaccines, individually or in combination, could have played a role in *some* cases of autism?" Many of our children develop quite normally and suddenly spiral downhill following an MMR or a DPT vaccine. Many become more and more affected and withdrawn with successive inoculations. There is indeed a correlation between the timing and severity of autistic symptoms and vaccination. Aren't the questions regarding the relationship between vaccines and autism meaningful, rational, educated and purposeful? Certainly, they are. Yet for many, there is a stark refusal to even ask, let alone investigate.

Conversely, look at the questions that oppose parents on this issue.

A question designed to *obfuscate* the discussion:

> "Why raise the issue of vaccines in autism, when vaccines have benefited society so profoundly?"

A question designed to *manipulate* the discussion:

> "Why be concerned about vaccine damage, when side effects are so rarely reported?"

A question designed to *complicate* the discussion:

> "Why be suspicious of a vaccine in autism, which is clearly a mental or genetic disorder?"

A question designed to *terminate* the discussion:

> "Why raise the issue of relatedness between autism and vaccines, when there is no causal proof?" (My favorite, because no one will fund the appropriate studies necessary to determine a causal relationship.)

These examples illustrate the kinds of questions that are designed not to *investigate* or *postulate*, but to obfuscate, complicate, contaminate, manipulate and even terminate the topic at hand. They *contribute nothing* to the answers or the solutions being sought.

Think how different the course of the last four decades would have been if the people who have pigeon-holed autism in various ways would have asked,

> "Do autistic children have any common underlying pathologies, outside of the brain, that could be the cause of their behaviors?"

> "How could we harness information on family histories, blood profiles, and other medical information in one place to look at potential common denominators in the physiology of autistic children?"

> "What environmental factors (including vaccines) could have possibly affected these children at the onset of their symptoms?"

> "How can we best facilitate and address the needs of these children and their families?"

> "Since we don't know what causes autism, how can we rule out any reasonable theory?"

"Do we know *everything* there is to know about autism? Is it possible that researchers just haven't looked in the right place yet to determine the cause?"

Think about how much more we might know, if *all* of our present-day doctors, educators, psychologists and specialists would entertain these same questions!

Just as there are beliefs and individuals that build up or tear down our efforts, our questions can sharpen our focus and our attitudes or they can leave us with more hopelessness. Our questions are the engines of our actions and they can be *Trail Makers* or *Rail Breakers*. The questions that we ask, individually, or collectively, set our agenda and our likelihood for finding answers about our children.

The integrity of our questions sets the stage for the information we receive. And never can we expect the right answers, from our facilitation partners, our doctors, our government officials, our educators, our researchers or ourselves, if we are asking the wrong questions or no questions at all, from the outset. Our questions can lead us to the aurora of empowerment or they can leave us on the dark side of Venus, in the shackles of autism, forever.

Below are some general everyday examples (not specific to any single philosophy or agenda) of what I've labeled *Rail Breakers* and *Trail Makers*. After taking a look at them, you will be able to determine in which category the questions you ask each day, belong.

Examples of *Rail Breakers*

1. What will we do if he/she doesn't recover?
2. Will my life always be this miserable?
3. Why did this have to happen to us/me?

4. Why can't he/she be just like all of the other children?

5. How am I ever going to handle this situation?

6. Why should I bother trying if autism is an incurable, untreatable disorder?

7. Why can't I have a social life?

8. Will this ever change?

9. How come nobody understands what I'm going through?

10. How come nobody comes to help?

11. Will I ever have the time for my other children?

12. Why doesn't someone find the answer to this illness?

13. What difference will my little voice make in a system so opposed to new thinking?

Examples of *Trail Makers*

1. How and what can I learn from my child's symptoms or from this medical test or evaluation that will positively direct my efforts and direction with my child?

2. How can this situation be used to benefit my other children, not just my child who is ill?

3. What changes can I implement in my child's diet that can only serve to help him/her?

4. What is one thing I can do or investigate or advocate for today that will move my child toward recovery?

5. What important clues presented themselves today that will help lead me in a positive plan of action for my child's educational or medical intervention?

6. What resource material can I be reading that will provide some of the answers for my child's recovery?

7. How can I show my autistic child that I love him (or her)?

8. What individuals in history, or whom I know personally, can I look toward as models of people who overcame challenges, and what can I learn from them?

9. What one positive thing can I do today to advance the awareness and/or progress of autism research? (Example: Write a letter to an educator, a government representative, CDC, physician, researcher, etc.)

10. What do I have to be grateful/thankful for today?

11. To whom in the autism community can I write a note of encouragement or thanks?

12. What one contribution can I make today toward my child's educational program?

13. What can I read or do today to help shape the right attitude and approach within myself?

14. What can I do today that would be fun with my child?

15. How can I build a better support team for my child?

16. What "seeds" can I plant today that I can cultivate over the next twelve-month period?

17. How can I positively impact the view that others have about autism?

18. Which interventions, educationally and biomedically, have had the best success, and are they relevant to my child?

19. How can I give the gifts of faith and hope to my child and family?

20. What medical tests will yield the greatest degree of information from which I can target a legitimate plan of action?

The scope and meaningfulness of our questions define the scope and meaningfulness of our research. Permit only meaningful questions in your discourse with others if you want to find answers for your child.

Chapter Sixteen

Empowerment Plan Step #8:
Looking for the Light

"You know more of a road by having traveled it than by all of the conjectures and descriptions in the world."

~ William Hazlitt

I will never deny my God-given, intuitive sense as a parent, and I will be confident in my observations and assessments of my own child. Furthermore, I will always look for the light - the connections, and the clues - from within my child to help direct the course of his recovery.

In the early 1970's, the famous musical composer Leonard Bernstein wrote and produced a work entitled "Mass." *Mass* was tremendously controversial. The subject matter of the production was a Catholic Mass as interpreted by Bernstein, who was Jewish.

The setting for the Mass was a simple church, filled with common, simple people. Bernstein used music, rock bands, singers and dancers to juxtapose the simplicity of the setting with the social tension of the decade and the anxieties of the clergy of the church. The celebrant of the Mass (the priest), and the parishioners of the church, led lives filled with disorder, confusion, and chaos. Bernstein used his music and the setting for the Mass to convey that peace and goodness can eventually transcend disorder and chaos. We, as mortal beings, have an active role in that process.

In perhaps the most emotional and poignant scene of the work, the celebrant of the Mass reveals his human side – fraught with pressure and doubt, besieged with anxiety, worry and introspection. As the Mass gets underway, the celebrant's anguish becomes fueled all the more, by parishioners who begin to chant "Dona-nobis-pacem" (give us peace). Their chants escalate to loud and furious proportions, until the parishioners are wild and out of control in their pleas to the celebrant. The celebrant cannot heed their requests for peace, however, painfully recognizing the limits of his own humanity.

As the celebrant becomes swept into the chaos, he takes a beautiful glass chalice – perhaps the only thing of extraordinary beauty in the simple sanctuary – and smashes it into tiny pieces in the middle of the Mass, in front of his chanting parishioners. It is a stunning moment, as the celebrant loses all composure and then leaves the scene in anguish and despair.

Later, the celebrant gathers enough courage to return to the now empty sanctuary. The clear and simple tones of a flute can be heard in the background. There lie the broken fragments of the beautiful chalice. The celebrant inspects the fragments of the chalice. He realizes that even in its broken state, he can see beautiful reflections of light in the pieces of glass before him. Some would see only ruin in the fragments of that broken chalice. The celebrant picks the pieces up and sees the clarity and the vision of what they could be, the vision of wholeness. In his ability to do so, he finds hope amidst in the shadows of life and the potential for reconciliation where things have been torn apart. Peace has finally come out of chaos, harmony out of cacophony.

Bernstein did not write about autism, but his message is no less our ally because of that. As parents, we have a vision that haunts us as it haunts no one else. We can see the chalice whole even through the broken pieces. If we were to allow others to convince us that the pieces in front of us are but a worthless pile of shards, destined to be pieced together to some degree of functionality at best, our children would never reach the wholeness of our vision. Yet that is exactly what we do when we sit by complacently and accept many of the current and past views about autism.

In the broken condition of autism, there is peace and light to be found. Among the clouds that surround them, there is the luminescence of our children that breaks through, often unexpectedly. Though we cannot predict when it will happen, we must look for it and treat it with reverence and a sense of high importance. The moments of light that peek through the darkness are our connections and clues to the underlying causes of our children's illness. The clues need to be treated reasonably and respectfully by us and by those who oversee our children's medical and educational well being.

For weeks following Parker's endoscopy and Secretin Challenge Test, one clue after the next, one beam of light after another, revealed itself from Parker's impaired body. Had we not used our better judgment, we would have been left, by many professionals, to simply shrug our shoulders and wonder forever what had produced Parker's sudden burst of tremendous improvement.

Fortunately for Parker, we embraced the hope amidst the hopelessness and eventually so did many very fine, caring, and selfless physicians. Truth transcended the doubt, and it validated the connection we had suspected. Of all of the steps to our plan of empowerment, our commitment to never deny our God-given, intuitive sense as parents and to be confident in our observations and assessment of our own child is the step for which, in retrospect, we are most grateful. The cost to have ignored those moments of brilliance from within Parker and our better, rational, intelligent judgment, would have been the sacrifice of our son's ultimate progress.

Be confident in your analysis and your observations of your own child! Look for the clues, the reflections of normalcy, of wellness, of promise that appear from time to time. Don't accept that they are unimportant and inherent aspects of your child's illness. Don't be intimidated by individuals who use words like "anecdotal" and "subjective" in condescending ways to describe your worthy assessments of your child. Look for connections and share them with others!

Do improvements or deterioration in your child follow dietary changes?

Do improvements or deterioration in your child follow periods of high temperature or fever?

Do improvements or deterioration in your child follow certain medication or supplements?

Do improvements or deterioration in your child follow specific educational intervention?

Do improvements or deterioration in your child follow seasonal changes?

Do improvements or deterioration in your child follow particular medical procedures?

There is hope within the fragments of autism! There is peace within the chaos. Harness the hope and the peace no matter how scattered or intermittent each may appear. As we look for these connections, these moments of light within the darkness, we will inspire the questions and the research that will eventually solve the mystery of autism itself.

Chapter 17

The Transformation:
Of Thinking, Of Acting, Of Autism

"There is one thing stronger than all the armies in the world: an idea whose time has come."

~ Victor Hugo

It has been five long and arduous years since Parker became ill. Every day one more bit of information has been uncovered, one more clue, one more connection has been revealed. Our journey will continue until a cure is found. We will never, ever quit.

The proponents of the myths of autism defend their beliefs passionately. So did the followers of medieval astrology. After medieval times, many battles were fought between those who believed in astrology and those who believed in rational science.[24] Likewise, some of the voices for the conventional beliefs about autism will not yield easily to the new voices of reason and progress, but we cannot allow the rational voices of reason and progress to be silenced any longer. Without such voices of reason to speak *for* them today, people with autism may remain silent for more generations to come.

One of my fellow parents, Mark Blaxill, recently offered these words regarding the increasing population of children stricken with autism:

"In the midst of an epidemic, one in which overwhelming evidence suggests multiple body systems are dysregulated, the medical community seems more absorbed in turf battles, research games and denial of the underlying problem than in helping our children and finding answers. Those professionals who are closest to finding real markers of the disease and showing real data are threatened, dismissed and attacked by their colleagues. The research programs move on with bizarre priorities and no sense of urgency. Many medical professionals, when challenged by parents for progress, retreat to the high ground of medical and research standards, but refuse to accept meaningful performance standards for the results they are delivering. They have no comprehensive theory of the cause of the disease, no comprehensive care-delivery model, no comprehensive model of treatment and effective intervention. Into this gaping vacuum, the parents are forced to intervene: driving the research agenda, organizing conferences, discovering therapies, mobilizing epidemiological research, fighting for care, conducting original research on their own. Make no mistake: this is an institutional performance failure of the highest magnitude."

We have politely protected the myths at great cost to our children and our families. In seeking change, we must realize that grand change will demand grand thoughts and grand actions.

We cannot be willing to continue walking in circles of darkness divided, if we want to stand in the lighted circle of progress, united in a meaningful cause, determined to find the cure.

The first few doors of change will open into walls of opposition and winds of resistance. Peeking through those walls are cracks of light and warmer currents of air. Those are our signs of the incredibly caring doctors, brilliant and savvy parents, forward-thinking, supportive educators and pioneering scientists and researchers who will eventually defy the myths. Rational, methodical science and thinking, professional and parental wisdom, will shine through and lead us forward, together. *And, as we refuse some of the counsel that our wisdom contradicts, some of the counselors will have no alternative than to reconsider.*

We cannot be the subjects in the Skinner boxes of hopelessness, indiscriminate about the crumbs we are given, marching in step as long as we are given *"something"* – especially when that *"something"* is ultimately worthless to our children's lives *today*. We must actively *stand up* and *speak out* for meaningful change. Change that puts biological causes at the forefront of funding and research. Change that encourages researchers to investigate physiology and evaluate potential biomedical treatments for our children. Change that demands not only more meaningful questions, but also straight answers and unbiased research from the institutions all around us. Change that recognizes and values educational settings and services that are appropriate to the needs of children besieged by autism. Change in the entire foundation and definition of autism.

Our responsiveness to the situation we face every single day defines the very fiber of the autism cause. *How* we respond will make us victims of our own cause, or creators of a new destiny – the cure.

Yes, for now we still remain on Venus. But, the question to ask each day as we awaken is, "Are we *trapped* here?" We can lift the clouds around us by becoming empowered. Our empowerment makes us *undeniably visible* to the rest of those people still living on Earth, and *incontrovertibly strong* as we stand together in positive action.

Beyond the clouds of autism, there are stars of hope and progress:

> ... *the stars of our children's improvements*

> ... *the stars of helpful, caring doctors and scientists*

> ... *the stars of compassionate, dedicated therapists and school officials*

> ... *the stars of facilitation partners*

> ... *the stars of triumph over false premises and old myths of autism, and*

> ... *the stars of truth in science regarding the physiology of autism.*

These stars become more obvious as we become empowered for positive, purposeful change within the autism community. Our empowerment is the hope and the light against the shadows of autism. It *is* the aurora on the dark side of Venus. From the aurora we can individually *see*, and *chart*, and *reach* the stars for our child. Further, as an empowered community, we begin to examine the *patterns of stars* and commonalities that emerge from sharing our individual experiences and wisdom with one another. These will inspire biomedical research, point to the causes and eventually to the cure for our children. In this way, the wisdom of our collective, empowered body will restore order to our children's physical bodies. The stars of hope and progress, our collective empowerment, and the wisdom of our body, will reveal a map of meaningful direction and a navigation guide away from autism. Our visions of wellness for our children will be realized, and together we will return back home.